Machines Against Measures

Machines Against Measures

Irene Sotiropoulou

BLOOMSBURY ACADEMIC
LONDON • NEW YORK • OXFORD • NEW DELHI • SYDNEY

BLOOMSBURY ACADEMIC
Bloomsbury Publishing Plc
50 Bedford Square, London, WC1B 3DP, UK
1385 Broadway, New York, NY 10018, USA
29 Earlsfort Terrace, Dublin 2, Ireland

BLOOMSBURY, BLOOMSBURY ACADEMIC and the Diana logo
are trademarks of Bloomsbury Publishing Plc

First published in Great Britain 2023

A catalogue record for this book is available from the British Library.

A catalog record for this book is available from the Library of Congress.

ISBN:	HB:	978-0-7556-3958-8
	PB:	978-0-7556-3959-5
	ePDF:	978-0-7556-3961-8
	eBook:	978-0-7556-3960-1

Series: Autonomy and Automation

Typeset by Integra Software Services Pvt. Ltd.

To find out more about our authors and books visit www.bloomsbury.com
and sign up for our newsletters.

Contents

Acknowledgements

This book might have been written by one person but in reality it would not have been possible if many more people did not play their part throughout the years.

There are the people who participate in the grassroots economic initiatives and who have done all the work that the book talks about. Without their efforts and thinking this book would not exist. Among them have been the research participants who have been willing to teach me about their activity and to whom I am deeply grateful.

I am grateful to the team that helped me and encouraged me to write this book: Dr Matthew Cole, who is the book series editor, Ms Atifa Jiwa, Ms Nayiri Kendir, Mr Tomasz Hoskins, Dr Michael Springer and Mr Peter Stafford, who have been the patient, understanding and supporting editors of this project and helped me with advice and comments, as well as Ms Adriana Brioso who designed the book cover and Ms Joanne Rippin and Ms Sophie Campbell, who helped me during the production process. I also thank an anonymous reviewer who helped a great deal with their comments and advice on a previous version of the manuscript.

Finally, some dear friends, they know who they are, whose support and encouragement have been essential for this book to be finalized. They were there when needed and were always thinking that this book has been a brilliant idea, even when I did not have the courage to believe it myself.

All deficiencies of this book are the sole responsibility of the author.

Part One

The non-mainstream modes of transaction and production and the quantity question

1

Introduction: The non-mainstream modes of transaction and production, or when what works in practice struggles to work in theory

When I decided to write this book, it was autumn 2019. The Coronavirus pandemic was about to start challenging our valuations and perceptions of quantity, revealing in one more telling way the structural problems of our economic system(s). My book, at that time, in the pre-pandemic era, had been decided to be a discussion about the measuring practices of people who try to organize themselves in order to be economically active but without doing the harm capitalism does to nature and humans.

The book would include findings from my research in Greece, from 2009 onwards, and would explore whether measuring practices that diverge from the capitalist ones are better, at least to support survival. And whether the use of digital technologies in order to perform those different measuring practices have a potential to support communities to cover their needs in a more egalitarian manner, at least temporarily – until better technologies are available.

In my research and also in my life in Greece I had seen how capitalism, in particular the capitalist restructuring after 2008, would use various ways of quantifying everyday life and politics in order to justify and impose exploitative policies and economic practices. Quantification in this context is a practice where everything is seen as identical to other things, and its main characteristic that might differentiate this everything from those other things is its quantity. In capitalism quantity is not of any type but usually and ultimately (that is, at the end or at the core of every measurement) it is represented by money, in most cases official currency, that is, currency sanctioned by state authorities.

This quantification is not the only one capitalism uses and it is much less the only quantification that human societies are using, can use or have used in the past. However, its character is fundamental because it creates a contrast and a distance between what money represents and the things that are represented by it. If we measure economic activity with money, any activity that does not support the increase of money is perceived as useless or harmful to economic activity. The trade-off that was represented in both discourse and practice in Europe and the United States, between 'the economy' and public health during 2020, has already been at work in Greece of the bailouts of banks and memoranda agreements since 2010. Neoliberal policies in Greece have devastated the public healthcare system to such an extent that a major part of the grassroots initiatives we are going to discuss in this book have been and still are social clinics and social pharmacies, which are grassroots-organized initiatives that provide free healthcare to whomever needs it. Therefore, capitalist quantification does not reduce quantities in our social and economic life that we need to use to survive. It only forces those quantities to exist in ways that do not reduce the money quantification of assets according to the perceptions adopted by those who hold most of the money.

Watching the same policies, and the outrageous idea that there can be a thriving economy while healthcare is not properly supported, taking over the wealthiest countries as a normality made me think that this book can be a call that we definitely need to talk, talk about quantities. We need to discuss how they are perceived, how they are counted, which of them are prioritized by policy-makers and why, and why the quantities that we (the people) think of as important (like the number of the Covid-19 deaths and the number of the healthworkers who got sick or died of Covid-19) are not treated as being as important as they should be. As we (the people) think they should be.

This book is not about Covid-19 and how the quantities used in the public debates revealed that there is a class struggle taking place right now about those quantities. I will be using examples related to the Coronavirus pandemic, but my focus will be on activities that took place before the pandemic. The critical years during which those activities took place were of not less importance for the communities that had to survive them. There have been casualties in Greece because of reductions in healthcare and general welfare expenditure since 2010, and there would have been even more if the grassroots schemes we discuss here did not exist.

Therefore, the book is about what people did to survive, in particular during what many people label as a 'crisis'. The 'crisis' in Greece has not ended yet and there is not any sound anticipation about when the economy will really recover. By 'recover' we (the people) mean when we will not need social clinics to treat people and when people will not be short of a day's meal. Quantities like GDP are not important to us (the people) if there are not enough hospitals, doctors and medicines for us (the people).

I am not going to discuss everything that people did to survive. There are many sources about Greece since 2010 for this. My focus is on specific organizing practices, which for the purposes of this book I call non-mainstream modes of transaction and production. By modes of transaction I mean the methods that people employ to allocate goods and services, as well as resources and labour among themselves, such as in a community. For example, using a currency to pay for food is a mode of transaction. By modes of production I mean the ways that people employ to decide what needs to be produced, by whom, for whom and under which conditions. For example, using a factory where workers work for a wage in order to produce cars that then the owner of the factory sells at a profit, is a mode of production. Modes of production and modes of transaction are quite complicated arrangements, because they have various levels of organizing, that include those from poor people, the ones who produce, buy and sell food, to big corporations that run international networks of foodstuff production and trade.

In this book, we are interested in modes of transaction and production that are not the usual ones, for example not all people participate in them and our legal and political systems do not really recognize them as important or valid. Our economic system is called capitalism, which means that the priority of the economic system is to create capital (accumulated privately owned money that is used to produce more profit, that is, more accumulated money). All economic decisions in capitalism have, in one way or another, as a main aim to increase the profits of capital, that is of the owners of capital, and increase capital as such and its ability to access (that is, to buy or command) other resources that are necessary for ensuring that profit. Not by coincidence, many of those other resources, like soil and water, are also needed for producing the things we need in our lives.

Prioritizing profits of capitalists over everything else is not a decision that is taken collectively, much less democratically. For example, the decision to allow international tourism to take place in summer and autumn 2020 (and 2021 and 2022) while the pandemic has been ravaging Europe was taken probably because capitalists of tourism preferred to have profits and not because health practitioners were advising that movement of populations during a pandemic would create more cases and casualties.

Non-mainstream modes of transaction and production therefore aim or aspire to prioritize other objectives of activity instead of capitalist profit. In this book, we are not interested in all non-mainstream modes of transaction and production, because we do not assume that all those modes are by definition better than capitalism. We are interested in the modes of transaction and production that aspire to create economic arrangements that are supportive of nature and human communities instead of harming them. Those modes are usually employed by social movements, communities or small organizations that try to implement their nature- and human-friendly principles through their activities.

In Greece, many grassroots organizations or schemes emerged since 2009 (before that date, this type of organizing existed but the number of organizations and their membership was very limited) that experimented and/or still experiment with those modes of production and transaction. Not every scheme did everything, in the sense that they focused on something more specific, like a need that had to be covered (for example healthcare or food) or a way of organizing together that needed to be explored (like a currency).

Therefore, under the term 'non-mainstream modes of transaction and production' in this book, there are various ways of arranging the production and distribution of goods and services, which range from the use of official currency to the use of other types of currencies or to non-monetary transactions altogether. Some of those ways of production and distribution also arrange productive efforts in ways by which people organize their production collectively and share their produce among themselves and with other people. In some cases, the sharing takes place without asking immediately for any reward. In other cases, the contribution back to the community or to the people who offered their produce and effort is arranged to take place according to rules that allow variability of the new contributions with respect to what those contributions can be and when they could be made. For example, in a non-monetary exchange network, the person who produces food might be able to offer produce only at certain times of the year, due to the seasonality of farming activities.

The types of the activities I examine are the following: parallel currencies are those accounting units that are created by the users themselves and which are used in their transactions instead of the official currency. Time banks are a type of parallel currency where the accounting unit is an hour of time. Therefore, each hour of work is equal to another hour of work, irrespective of the content of the work involved in the two cases. Exchange networks are collective arrangements where people transact without the use of a collectively set accounting unit or without the use of accounting unit at all. Free bazaars and free networks are initiatives in which people give to other people things that they do not need and they take things they need when those are offered within the initiative.

Sui generis schemes also rely on non-monetary exchange or turn other items (like artworks or used mass transport tickets) into payment means. Solidarity structures like social kitchens, clinics or educational initiatives are those which provide for free necessities like food, healthcare and education, through collective arrangements of people who work together to make this provision possible to their communities. Similar organizing is used in collective cultivation groups, where people cultivate land together and share their produce in the same manner (Sotiropoulou 2012a, 2016a, 2016b).

There are also other solidarity activities that are undertaken in emergency situations, like grassroots efforts to support refugees and people who have been affected by severe disasters. In this latter case, the effort is not strictly localized by definition, as resources and support need to be mobilized from one area or region to another. In those same cases, the use of machines is even more prominent given the limited time that is available and the extent of the solidarity that needs to be provided in a short time span.

Of all those activities, what interests us here is the use of digital technologies by these schemes and their members and the ways they are understanding quantity and measures. An example: what we want to see is not whether the prioritization of healthcare by a social clinic is a better choice than prioritizing the profits of banks (that are usually bailed out with public funds). In this book our position is that healthcare, access to adequate food (food sovereignty included), a thriving ecosystem and strong democratic communities are much better choices than capitalist profit. We are not going to discuss whether capitalism is a good system or a system that could be good – because it is not a good economic system and cannot be improved.

What we are going to discuss is in what ways the prioritization, for example, of healthcare, by a social clinic, implies the use of other quantities, other measures and other technologies. Or if the measures, quantities or technologies are similar to the capitalist ones, in what ways those are used that makes the prioritization of healthcare possible (if it is made possible). We are going to explore this aspect of the practices of grassroots schemes because we see that quantity is central in capitalism. But this seems equally to be the case in any other economic arrangement we want to support. We need to examine whether we are talking about the same quantities, whether the use of the same technologies for measuring is problematic, and whether we can have non-capitalist and possibly non-patriarchal measures, quantities and technologies.

Why are quantities and measures so important? Can we live without them? We shall see in the next chapters that in some cases, quantities might not be important and measuring is skipped in certain aspects of economic activity. In some other cases, however, quantities are important, and we need to think about what measures we need and how to use them. Along with the measures or the non-use of measures, there comes the use of technologies, in particular the digital technologies. Capitalism uses them; what do the grassroots initiatives do in that respect?

The decision to write this book emerged from the finding that all this activity is really under-theorized if not disdained and erased both as practice and as theory-thought. Moreover, the activity as an aspiring non-capitalist and possibly non-patriarchal undertaking has not been seen from the point of view of the people who work so hard to establish the grassroots schemes and to achieve their goals. That is, we have no theory from the point of view of economies that are not or try not to be capitalist and patriarchal. Obviously, critical theory is very useful in that respect, because we can see the social struggle taking place within and through those grassroots schemes and place it within a broader historical and economic context.

However, once we accept that capitalism does not work for the majority's benefit and that we need other, better, economic structures, it is not easy to proceed with our thoughts in the same systematic way as the critique to capitalism can be done. The work that people in all those initiatives have done, even when there are problems, is a material, grounded starting point for both our thoughts and practices. Both their achievements and their problems are extremely useful in order to develop our thoughts without ending up in wishful thinking.

That we do not have adequate theory or systematic thought over all those grassroots practices is not a problem of the practices themselves. That many of those practices might challenge a lot of theories, not only the neoliberal ones, but also those standing on the progressive and egalitarian side, is exactly what we need at this moment. We can learn from what has worked well in practice, even if we did not anticipate it in theory. But we cannot learn from what has worked well in theory if we have not tried it in practice, to see whether we miss some aspect of it while we anticipate wishfully its function in advance.

All the schemes I will refer to here have been created on their own initiative, that is, not within the framework of any research project. My research was not action research. I was participating in various initiatives, to the extent that I as a researcher was allowed to, but my research was not about creating any economic structure as such. It was about documenting what was happening. I was learning from the people who created and worked in the initiatives, because I was not only lacking theory but also words to describe what was happening. For this reason, you will see that the book does not employ any specific terminology, because we do not have any. I use a lot of examples to present my thoughts because this is how my thoughts have been generated.

I do not aspire to create any big theory with this book. However, I aspire to make sure that even small theories that might come out of it can be quite well grounded on real economic phenomena. Even if a big theory was possible at this stage, it would be a collective project that cannot be substituted by a book.

The next chapter (chapter two) presents the general theoretical background of the book, that is, what we mean by capitalist patriarchy and what quantity has to do with this economic, social and political system. Chapter three is also a theoretical chapter that focuses on the political economic implications of quantity and quantification, and on the relationship of quantification to violence. Chapter four presents my approaches concerning how I have done research on those topics so far with an emphasis on the problem of quantitative methods that we have when we want to understand grassroots economic activities that aspire to create egalitarian economic arrangements.

Chapter five is the first chapter of the second part of the book and is dedicated to how quantity and measures are perceived and practised in various grassroots economic initiatives. Chapter six explores time as a measure of quantity in the grassroots schemes, and chapter seven explores the question of value. Because, whether we like it or not, the quantification and measures are used in order for communities to get some grasp of value understandings or in order to support the values that the communities prefer. Chapter eight is dedicated to the uses of the digital technologies in grassroots economic initiatives, and chapter nine explores the use of technological tools again, but this time through the broader prism of machines as means of production for modes of production that could be non-capitalist.

The third part of the book starts with an overview (chapter ten) of the neoliberal policies in Greece during the last twelve years and how they affected the perceptions of quantities and measures. Chapter eleven discusses how the grassroots use of measures and technologies was an attempt to support social (and natural) reproduction within that broader neoliberal context that worked against nature and human communities' survival. Chapter twelve discusses how capitalist patriarchal pressures and practices can still be found in the grassroots schemes, and how we need to be aware of the contradictions of the grassroots economic activities if we really want to achieve their aims. Chapter thirteen concludes the book by discussing how we are in the impossible situation where we lack adequate technologies and quantity perceptions and we need, instead of giving up, to create them from scratch. We are in the impossible historical moment where in the midst of a vast global environmental, healthcare, economic and political crisis, we have to experiment with what we have at hand in order to find what we would like to create.

2

Theoretical background: Capitalist patriarchy, quantification and the alternatives to capitalism

The grassroots economic initiatives that I described in the previous chapter have emerged and functioned during a specific time at a specific geographical place. For many types of these initiatives, there is no theory at all. Moreover, there is not enough research about them and we have no clear picture about what is happening in countries other than Greece with reference to those forms of economic activity and organizing. For this reason, it would not be wise to theorize by assuming that those economic activities exist in exactly the same manner in other countries.

It would be equally mistaken to consider Greece as a special case of grassroots economic activity, simply because it happens that we have more information and research for that country about various initiatives of this character. After all, the economic traits of Greece are not unique in the Balkans and the Eastern Mediterranean and one would need a broader investigation to identify this activity within its geographical context.

Context is fundamental to understanding this activity in general and even more necessary to understand the economy in all cases. Just as with the rest of the economic phenomena, I understand the grassroots economic schemes described in the previous chapter as taking place within a specific historical time period and geographical space, where the main and prevailing political-social-economic system is capitalist patriarchy.

By 'prevailing' I mean that the economic system is the one that is reflected in the main institutions of a society and the one that the elites, or those who have the most economic and political power, have the ability to impose on society. Having a prevailing economic system means that there might be other economic systems coeval to it, that is, existing at the same time in the same economy. However, the non-prevailing economic systems are not reflected in the main institutions of a society to the same extent and in the same way as the prevailing system. Definitely, the non-prevailing economic systems are not the preferred ones by the most powerful, even if in some cases the most powerful might use (or abuse) parts of those non-prevailing economic systems for their own benefit.

Prevailing economic system and non-prevailing economic systems might be articulated together in a symbiotic relationship or they might be antagonistic. The non-prevailing systems might also be symbiotic or antagonistic with each other. And of course, in the antagonism among non-prevailing economic systems, some might coordinate themselves with the prevailing system, while other economic systems might be found in antagonistic situations with both the prevailing economic system and the other non-prevailing ones. An example would be an articulation of feudal economic practices (producers with a formal or informal status of slavery or serfdom or debt bondage) with contemporary capitalism (wage workers) while non-patriarchal egalitarian practices struggle to keep going in times and in a context of such a feudal-capitalist articulation (for example, people in quasi-slavery conditions organizing to demand worker rights or joining a collective production initiative in order to avoid poverty and unemployment).

For this book, patriarchy is a central concept of economic understanding and analysis. We usually think of patriarchy as a social system, sometimes as a political system. It is, however, an economic system as well, because it defines, among other things, the relationship of individuals and communities to resources and to each other as economic actors.

In other words, patriarchy is understood as a political economic system and not only as a social system that affects the economy in collateral ways. The economic system of patriarchy is based not only on the power of men over women in general, but on the power of certain men entitled to private property, while having the means to exclude everyone else from this property. In patriarchy property is understood as existing in land, women, children, and on all beings and things that patriarchy perceives as possible and necessary to become properties (Courville 1993, Fraser 2013a, 2013b, Federici 2013, Ehrenreich & English 1978, Bennholdt-Thomsen et al. 1988, Barker & Kuiper 2003, Eisenstein 1979, Lerner 1986, Mayes 2005, Zelizer 1994).

Patriarchy in reality understands property as a relationship that can exist with everyone and everything around. Practically, it understands property as the only relationship that can exist with self, people and things, including nature. That there have been patriarchies where property was delimited in one or another way does not make the economic system of patriarchy less prone to making everything a property. It means that we need to check what resistances patriarchy found in a certain economic context, and in what ways and for which reasons some people and some things were exempted from being properties.

The people whom patriarchy exempts from being properties are the property owners. In each patriarchy there are specific social groups that have property over everything else and everyone else. In some cases, the property over humans and nature can take an explicit form, such as legislation that permits slavery and land property. In other cases, the property over humans and nature can be implicit: formal laws do not accept property over humans or over commons, but the set of formal rules and their implementation, along with social attitudes, impose such property *de facto*. An example would be natural sites or the climate system(s), that are formally commons, but in practice have been privatized by being destroyed by pollution emitted by private companies. It is not a coincidence that the owners of properties tend usually to be men or substitutes of men (like corporations). The reason is that in patriarchy the human model of an owner and free person is male (hooks 1984, 1997, Agathangelou & Ling 2006, Fraser 2013a, Federici 2004, Borneman 1975, Cassano 2009, Dallacosta & James 1975, Graeber 2006, Mayes 2005).

The important point concerning property in patriarchy is that the means for protecting, that is, excluding others from, property is violence. In the economic system of patriarchy the entitlement to violence is attributed to certain people only or to their substitute of political power (the local lord or the state). Violence is central in patriarchy, that is, violence is institutional (Bey 2021, hooks 1984, 1997, Federici 2004, Mies 1998, Peterson 2003, Ehrenreich & English 1973). In the economic system of patriarchy, violence acquires an economic character even if an incidence of violence does not seem to have direct economic motives. That is, violence against nature by 'indifference' is still violence that degrades the ecosystem at the expense of everyone and to the benefit of those who pollute, even if the polluters are just tourists having fun at a beach. Not having to do the care work of non-polluting is an economic benefit for those who tour and even more for the tour operators (that is, the capitalists) who make profits out of those who tour.

Apart from that, the basic institutions of patriarchy (private property over land, women and human bodies in general, the state, the exclusivity of rights to violence, and possibly money) are the core of each patriarchal economic system. In reality, patriarchy is defined by those economic institutions and not only by any gender struggle or conflict between sexes as such. After all, in patriarchy women are not perceived as equals to men, able or legitimated to wage any struggle against the patriarchs. That patrilineal kinship (defined through men's lineage) and its non-kinship replications are used to support those economic institutions does not make the institutions less economic. Just like the use of matriliny (kinship arranged on the basis of women's lineage) in some cases by patriarchy to support those patriarchal economic institutions, does not make the institutions less patriarchal.

Capitalism is therefore a version of patriarchy. I have just explained that the main economic institutions that we still have today as central in our economy are the patriarchal ones. In capitalism, the patriarchal economic institutions are arranged in such a way in order to give priority to money and its accumulated form (capital). The arrangement attributes to capital and to its owners and institutional proxies (like corporations and state authorities) all entitlements to violence so that this priority is maintained, enhanced and well serving the owners of capital. Because capital in capitalism is the property type *par excellence*, all properties are seen as capital (to be disposed of for more profit and capital) and all humans and nature are seen as resources and capital (to be disposed of for more profit and capital).

An example is the perception of natural capital or human capital in neoliberal economies, while we know from Marx's critique that capital means 'dead labour'. By 'dead labour' is meant the human effort that has already been exerted and propertied (in the form of money or in the form of monetized means of production) by a certain individual instead of being owned by the people who performed the labour (Marx 1992).

On the institutional and systemic levels, this type of economic system (patriarchy) and even more its contemporary form (capitalist patriarchy) needs certain perceptions of quantity in order to turn into discourse and symbolic communication the core idea that there is property and it belongs to certain people. Those same perceptions of quantity are also necessary to represent someone or something as property. For example, we have the price of a footballer's contract and explicit news reports that a football team 'bought' or 'acquired' an athlete from another football team. Another example is the assignment of prices or monetary values on public goods, so that they can be sold. Even if it is not to be sold, the priced public good is integrated into a hierarchy of monetary values, among the fortunes of tycoons, the government budgets and the defence expenditures of each state.

Within this context, capitalist patriarchal perceptions and practices of quantity and measure are arranged to normalize the devaluation of production performed by nature and by subordinate groups (women, groups of people who defy heteronormative arrangements, workers, colonized and neo-colonized peoples). Without this devaluation it is impossible to create a somehow coherent system of properties and of profits out of them. That is, if the work performed by women at home is considered to be of high value in capitalism, then women must be compensated for that work, otherwise capitalism must explain why this work remains unpaid. Even if women are not considered to be autonomous workers (capitalism is patriarchy, after all), capital owners will have to pay wages that reflect the whole reproduction costs of the workers they employ in the workplace (men or women), and not only the reproduction costs of the worker they have a contract with.

The same, and to an even more extractive extent, is happening with reference to the value of labour performed by workers who do not belong to the capital owners group (which group consists of usually white, of European descent, heterosexual – by performance at least – and middle-class males). They often belong to communities that have faced colonialism and were/are subjected to discrimination based on (the construction of) race in the past or still face neocolonialism and racism in the present. Their contributions and labour are deemed to be of minimal if of any value at all. This is very convenient for capitalist companies (usually coming from former colonial countries) to make huge profits by taking resources and labour from those peoples (whether they are living in countries in Europe and the US or within the states that were colonized in the past) and their countries. Race has been constructed and weaponized exactly for creating exploitative processes that transcend class and gender and reproduce the economic system as both capitalist and patriarchal. As hooks (1984, 1997) names it, this is a white supremacist capitalist patriarchy and the question whether capitalist patriarchy could avoid being white supremacist is a hypothetical one, the answer to which is necessarily marked by the actual historical material realities of that economic system (Davis 2011, Emmanuel 1976, Robinson 2000, Nembhard 2014, Rodney 1981).

The main way to achieve all these devaluation processes is to assign an unproductive or passive role to the human and non-human beings (including nature) in the process of production. *Unproductive* means that all those people are considered not to produce anything of value. That is, patriarchy, and capitalist patriarchy in particular, counted their contributions as having zero value or around zero value. It also means that the capital owners (which are patriarchal or patriarchal proxies) are the ones who produce. That is, capitalist patriarchy counted the capital owners' contributions and found them to be of utmost importance and volume for the production process. In that way, assigned/constructed passivity but also non-productivity take a very quantitative character, reflected in assumed values that are assigned through processes of power exertion – the property ownership and the violence we mentioned above.

The unproductive-passive role is therefore assigned to women (conflated with nature in all patriarchal systems) but also to all subaltern social groups or peoples, especially the poor, the colonized, the dark-skinned, the having-'other'-cultures peoples. Assigning a non-productive or under-productive role to various subordinate groups, affects measuring practices and the types of measures used for disciplining them.

In that way, we have mutually reinforcing quantifications and practices of deprivation: people are not able to have means of production available and this lack of property (or access to it) means that they are unable to produce enough for themselves or to negotiate better valuations for their work. The ownership of a machine or production tool defines who takes a major part, or even the whole value, of anything that is produced. And because the value of what is produced (that is, the wealth produced) goes to the owners of the machine, those who are not owners of the machine do not have any chance of owning a machine of their own, because their income is too low, because their work is not deemed to be productive enough, because they did not own a machine in the first place.

Through those measurings of value, the property institutions are reproduced and, along with them, the exploitation and injustice the patriarchal system entails. If we are talking about capitalist patriarchy, the reproduction of the system relies to an important extent on those quantifications, that is, the perceptions of the values that are created, and on perceptions about who owns those values and what comparisons of wealth those values allow.

Measuring value in capitalism is done through money (and through money only, in reality) and this measuring contributes to the reproduction of capitalism. Whatever cannot be measured in money is deemed not to have any value. Whatever can be measured in money is deemed to be comparable with any other money. That is, the monetary value of the ocean can be compared to the monetary value of the assets of a capitalist. The end result is that for the people who are not owners of money and means of production, the comparison presents them as of less value in general and of less potential for value in particular. In reality, the measurings in capitalist patriarchy allow extraction of value from these people who own neither money nor means of production. In some cases this extraction of value takes place at an absolute level, in most cases in the form of surplus value (Waring 1999, Won Werlhof 2007, Picchio 2005, Scholz 2014, Dalla Costa & James 1975, Federici 2013, Eisenstein 1979, Bennholdt-Thomsen et al. 1988, Albritton 2003).

Nature receives a similar treatment in this case. First, work performed by nature is erased under the perception of nature as non-productive, waiting for the entrepreneurial capitalist patriarchal agent (male, heteronormatively behaving, middle class, property owner, white-European descent) to make it productive. Second, anything that exists in nature is perceived as existing with the purpose of being used by humans and in particular by capitalists (Bennholdt-Thomsen et al. 1988, Mies & Shiva 1993, Von Werlhof 2007). If it cannot be used by capitalists for any reason (for example, it cannot easily be turned into property and then cut into pieces and sold as a commodity), it can be destroyed by other activities of capitalist patriarchy in an indirect way, as it is done with ecosystems through pollution or climate change. That is, climate cannot become property at this stage of capitalism (and hopefully, never will), which means that capitalist patriarchy does not see it as important to protect, but possible, instead, to be continually destroyed by capitalist economic activity. The trade-off I mentioned in the first chapter is again at work: 'the economy' is considered to be more important than climate, because 'the economy' increases the money and all quantities represented by it; while climate is seen only as an annoying disturbance to the economy, that is, a problem that costs money as if it is external to economic activity. In real terms, climate is an essential production factor that determines any economy.

In the quest of capitalist patriarchy to use nature more extensively and more intensively for the purpose of capitalist profits, the means of production, and in particular the technology that is available in each case, is of utmost important. The extraction of oil became possible because of certain technology that made oil a central energy source for capitalism. The technology of extraction and use of a part of nature (usually defined as a natural resource) enables human societies, but mostly capitalism, to quantify that part of nature and then to be able to extract profit from it, also in a highly quantified form. How much oil is available underground is a quantitative question that was meaningful once the technology was available to extract and use the oil, in combination with the demand for it in the economy.

Capitalist patriarchy in early 21st century is using digital technologies to monetize, that is, connect to monetary value, other quantities that it would have been unthinkable to monetize some decades ago. We have technologies for monetizing mood at work, or internet visibility of one's labour performance. We have technologies for monitoring and disciplining that, even if they do not increase use-value as such, nor even the workers' productivity, increase the value of the economic system of capitalist patriarchy. Because, through that discipline, the capital owners are acquiring more power to command labour, paid and unpaid, and the subordinate groups are even more dependent on capitalists' means of production to make a living. To this one would add the exploitation of people's leisure time and social relationships by capitalists for free or, worse, by extracting value from labour that is presented as leisure and socializing activity

(Moore et al. 2018, Beer 2016, Lanier 2018, McNamee 2020, Supiot 2017, Yeung 2018, Zuboff 2019).

Within this context, the measuring practices and the use of digital technologies in non-mainstream transaction and production modes are taking the ambivalent character that all activities in capitalist patriarchy take: are those activities reproducing the system or dismantling it? And if both answers are possible, what are the characteristics that differentiate each outcome of those activities? These are the questions to discuss in parts two and three of this book.

The important thing to note at this point is that capitalist patriarchy and its obsessive prioritization of money and capital and their measurement, but also their being made the measures of everything else, has led to severe reproduction crises. By reproduction I mean all activities that contribute and make sure that human society will survive to the next day, year and century. We usually distinguish between biological and social reproduction but, in reality, when we talk about reproduction, all reproduction is social and biological at the same time. A human needs food to survive, but the acquiring of food and the mere act of eating is a social act.

Social reproduction, however, has one more meaning: it also comprises the reproduction of social and economic systems. In other words, when someone is eating in capitalist patriarchy, that person is probably reproducing capitalist patriarchy – because they probably have to acquire food through capitalist patriarchal routes of food production and distribution. Whether some people might not be reproducing capitalist patriarchy through eating or through other activities of theirs is the big question about resistance to capitalist patriarchy and a big question in this book, too.

Use of capitalist valuations, that is, use of measures that count the values that capitalist patriarchy is interested in, is fundamental for the social reproduction of capitalist patriarchy. The technologies that facilitate those valuations and measuring of values are also part of that reproduction process. Some of those technologies that are used for this purpose have been created with this purpose in mind (of the capitalist), that is, to quantify what capitalist patriarchy needs to have quantified so that capitalist patriarchy is reproduced as a system.

Nevertheless, reproduction of an economic system is not the same as the reproduction of human societies, much less the reproduction of nature. They can be in a complementary relationship, that is, the reproduction of an economic system can support reproduction of ecosystems and human societies. But they can also be in contradiction. That is, an economic system can be detrimental to human societies and nature. An example is capitalist patriarchy. Patriarchal economic systems in general have not been very helpful to human societies – this is probably why we have experienced various forms of patriarchy, with various versions, that were more or less patriarchal. That is, people were trying to get rid of or mitigate a harmful economic system and in that way various forms of patriarchy were formed throughout history. Capitalist patriarchy, however, seems to have been the most destructive version of patriarchy we have seen in history so far.

In the early 21st century we can already talk about a global reproduction crisis, with nature and poor people being in danger every day (or killed/eliminated if needed for capitalist expansion). By *reproduction crisis* we mean that the economic system cannot effectively reproduce itself, and the society cannot effectively reproduce itself at the same time. The problem we have with capitalist patriarchy is that as an economic system, in order to be reproduced, it needs to do it at the expense, and by risking or decreasing the capabilities of reproduction, of nature and society. That is, capitalist patriarchy reproduced and reproduces itself by destroying natural and human livelihoods. In 2022 we are already at a point where the destruction has reached such a level and intensity that the reproduction of both society and the prevailing economic system is at stake (Barker & Feiner 2010, Caffentzis 2002, Ehrenreich 2002, Kurz 2014, Peterson 1997, 2010, Trenkle 2014, Zelizer 1994).

Even the so-called advanced capitalist countries are unable to reproduce themselves, in terms of adequate nutrition, health care and other care work of their population, without devastating other countries for extracting resources and cheap labour from them and without devastating the worker classes of all countries, even in the countries who are 'advanced' (that is, in terms of capitalism, those that have high GDP). The Covid-19 pandemic proved that things had been worse than anyone could have imagined. We need to understand that in times of reproductive crisis the structural problems are more related to the class and other social groups one belongs to rather than to what country one lives in. For example, even in countries like the UK and USA, those who were mostly affected were the poor people, but even more, the poor people who are also Black, Indigenous, immigrants, belong to various ethnic minorities, or to certain age groups or to certain groups with disabilities or health issues.

In that sense, if we are facing a situation where the reproduction of societies and of nature are in danger, we need to see grassroots economic activity through that prism. There is much discussion about alternatives to capitalism and how, by doing anything that is not capitalist (or at least seems to be not capitalist), you are destabilizing capitalism or at least the belief that capitalism is all that there is (Gibson-Graham 2006). However, if the question is about ensuring that nature and human societies will survive, and also that this is done without putting the burden on the poorest or the most vulnerable, then the situation and the related questions are more complex. Destabilizing our perception of capitalism is not enough in an emergency.

In the same way, we need to be careful, no matter how much we need optimism, when we see technology as a panacea to our environmental, economic and political problems (Bastani 2019, Dutta & Mia 2009, Dyer-Witherford 2013, Mayer-Schönberger & Cukier 2013, Mayer-Schönberger & Ramge 2018). This is after all an approach that existed one or two centuries ago, and it did not help to create the technologies that would avoid climate change, for example. Technology on its own cannot change an economic system. The material realities of capitalism and patriarchy are more complex and deeper than just planning with good faith a new economic arrangement, although we would like the process to be this smooth (Morozov 2013, 2019, mcm_cmc 2015,

Mostafa 2019, Saros 2014). We need to ask questions based on the material relations that we face and that we would like to establish instead of taking technology, nature and humans as we know (and use) them now for granted.

One set of questions is related to what is really reproduced by which process. Another set of questions is how the resilience of capitalism but also of patriarchy (which is a quite ancient and also evolving economic system) will not be once more based on the reproductive capacities of those who are oppressed by this same economic system. A third set of questions is related to how capitalist patriarchy that cannot easily reproduce itself is affected by and affecting the grassroots initiatives that we examine in this book.

All those questions are very important, but the book will focus on a very specific aspect of them: quantity and how digital technologies are used to express or use quantity and measures. Therefore, in this book, we are not looking for alternatives to capitalism as such – although we hope that some of the practices presented here might be good examples of what people collectively can do to disentangle their economic activity from the prevailing economic system and also fight back. We are looking to explore the quantitative practices, and if any of them appear to be non-capitalist or non-patriarchal, so much the better.

3

Theory again: Is measuring a form of violence?

We have seen in the previous chapter how violence is central in establishing and reproducing patriarchy and capitalist patriarchy. We also examined how patriarchy and capitalist patriarchy are very good at devaluing any labour and contribution they need for their reproduction. Those same forms of labour and contributions also happen to coincide with contributions that are needed for the reproduction of society and nature, irrespective of patriarchy.

We have also seen that patriarchy and, even more, its capitalist form uses quantification and measures in order to facilitate its reproduction in other ways. One way is the standardization of quantities that are important for capitalist patriarchy, for example, quantities of commodities or within commodities. Another example is time, in particular labour time and socially necessary labour time.

By *socially necessary labour time* we mean the time a person needs to spend on average in order to produce a certain item or service. The average is not a person's average but an aggregate average of the people of a society making that same effort. Obviously, in an economic system where the value of the effort of workers is contested, the socially necessary labour time for producing, e.g. shoes, is also contested. The owners of capital want to reduce the socially necessary labour time for the production of shoes or, if this is not possible, to increase the labour time or the labour intensity used for the production of shoes without rewarding the workers for this, that is, to use time as a unidirectional measure to extract more wealth from the workers. The workers on the other hand want to limit this extraction of wealth, either by getting better wages when the socially necessary labour time is reduced in production or by keeping the working hours within limits that allow them to rest and reproduce themselves and their social lives outside the workspace. Therefore, if there is a social struggle in society, this also affects the perception of how much time is needed to produce anything (Marx 1992, vol. 1).

Given that value in capitalism is expressed through monetary means because this facilitates the prioritization of capital and its owners, the class struggle is also related to the ways, not only the quantities, that money will or will not circulate in the economy (Campbell 2005, Likitkijsomboon 2005, Marx 1992 vols 1 and 3). This has important implications for and from all activities that avoid using official currency or any type of currency, as we shall see in the following chapters of the book. Moreover, there are other ways of using quantities in favour of capitalist patriarchy. One is to discard the quantities that are not favourable to the argument that the capital owners want to make. For example, for decades now we have known very well the quantities related to ecosystem destruction and to climate change. There is also an effort to quantify values of ecosystems in the (desperate) attempt to speak the language of capitalism in order to persuade people about protecting the environment, despite the fact that ecosystems are priceless and do not exist for humans only in the first place (Ackerman & Heinzerling 2001). However, all those quantities together are never taken as seriously as the quantities of profits or GDP growth. It is the same with measuring cases, casualties and people with post-Covid-19 impairment: no matter how clearly the numbers show the magnitude of the problem, those quantities still seem to be unimportant in many countries for making decisions that would protect the health of the citizens and the ability of healthcare systems to cope with the pandemic.

There is no intention to reduce the importance of using quantitative tools and statistics in order to support arguments that sustain worker social struggles. Quite the opposite, as an economist I cherish all efforts to use quantity and quantitative methods in ways that challenge exploitation and environmental degradation (Bruno et al. 2014,

Diaz-Bone & Didier 2016, Saltelli 2020, Saltelli et al. 2020). However, I am reluctant to discuss digital technologies and measuring processes as generic in a society full of class struggle and exploitation at the expense of the majority. After all, there is not much to argue about hybrid (ambivalent or balanced) relationships with technology (Dorrestijn 2012), while the question is always who, that is, which social group, is creating and/or using which technology for which purpose.

Another method of using quantities in favour of capitalist patriarchy is to attribute value or to quantify by priority what is important for suppressing resistances in society. In that way, finance, financiers, various investment funds and a range of banking products are highly valued, not only because they represent capital accumulation and capital owners but also because they are disciplinary structures at the expense of the rest of the economy, whose actors might not be happy enough to sustain capital as a priority. We will see the investment in police equipment and personnel again in chapter ten. But what the financial capital sector has done in particular since 2008 is to create an institutional framework of disciplining worker classes while wealth has been concentrated in the hands of various sections of the capitalist class (Wilmott & Orrell 2017). In reality, the police have been implementing this discipline in a more tangible way.

There is no doubt that quantification technologies give police departments huge opportunities to exert violence on worker classes and any other social groups that are both needed in urban centres in order to produce (both goods and the urban space itself) but are also required to be disciplined to the extreme so that the capitalist classes do not need to share wealth or means of production with them. That the quantification might be adopted in an effort to depersonalize criminal procedures and create some limitations to otherwise extensive powers of the judiciary or the policing services does not make the use of quantitative tools less problematic (Automating Banishment 2021, Espeland & Vannebo 2007, Foucault & Simon 1991, Morozov & Bria 2018).

Thus, that discipline, which is very violent and oppressive, is bound to quantities, because it is related to economic measures and to debt agreements that bind the state, the citizens, the banks and the investors (or 'investors'). Without those quantities, reflected in documents, or usually through digital registers between banks, it would have been impossible to construct a narrative that would support austerity in the EU since 2009 and the various debt bailout agreements in Greece since 2010. Greece bailed out the local private banks with public money and then the government debt got astray. As a consequence, the government (and the country) had to borrow in addition to the regular government debt, which made the debt unsustainable in practice (Glenn 2019: 153–192).

In other words, the quantities that were used to institutionalize the diversion of workers' wealth (whether private or collective, that is, reflected in state services) to the capitalist class have been weaponized against workers in a situation that took the form of a class war. If people think that class war is an exaggeration, the police brutality inflicted on those protesting against austerity in Greece in various cases needs to be explored as something that is not class war on the one hand (why not?), but is not class peace on the other. Before and during the use of physical violence, the institutional violence and discursive violence was there to curb resistances or at least to frame the whole situation as an unavoidable punishment for those who in reality never made any decision about the banking system or the government budget.

This is one more example of the already highly quantified framework of the contemporary state apparatus, which cannot provide social services or administer any situation without putting the population, in particular the worker classes, under surveillance; or under policies deriving from biased or erroneous understanding based on quantifications that have limited power to represent the reality that the state wants to administer (Berend 2005, Porter 1995, 2012), but which probably have a very strong connection to the reality the state wants to create.

The critique concerning the uses of quantity and accounting methods to discipline a society that is under metric control and governed through measuring is something that this book takes for granted as existing knowledge (Cowton & Dopson 2002, McKinlay & Pezet 2010, Mirowski & Nik-Khah 2017). In reality, the problems we have with quantity and measurement are quite deeper and older than the last decades, as the previous chapter showed. We are talking about a certain way of organizing societies in patriarchy and the last centuries in most parts of the world. We are experiencing a very intensified form of patriarchy, that is (colonial) capitalism, which affects all aspects of social life and various civilizational traits (Chandler & Fuchs 2019, Crosby 1998, Giblin & Doctorow 2022, Duncan 1984, Lave 1984, Mennicken & Salais 2022, Muller 2018, O'Neil 2016, The Sarai Programme 2003, Supiot 2017, Yeung 2018).

The fear that the use of technologies will replace human labour along with the value of it has been a very common critique of capitalist technologies since 19th century. There are divergent views about the ability of machines and their quantification potential to replace humans or their ability to resist (Arntz et al. 2016, Cole 2018, Petit 2015, Large 2018, Lohmann 2020). The important point is that the metrification of production and distribution processes has indeed allowed capital owners to extract more value from workers by forcing them to participate in their own metrification. Metrification further alienates the workers through the process of quantifying effort while depriving it of any meaning for the worker or their community (Graeber 2018, Moore & Robinson 2016, O'Neill 2016/2017).

Major contributions to the understandings of disciplining through numbers and quantifying technologies have been made by Foucault (1988, 1995), who explained through historical analysis how control and difficult-to-escape surveillance passes through measurement and quantity. When Foucault was writing, the management methods used today in order to account, analyse and direct production and distribution in a quantifiable manner did not exist, along with the technologies that are available today even to the lowest level of management. Financial quantification intensified in early 21st century. At the same time, the technologies that support the accumulation of capital through the quantifying management methods at work were developed with exactly this controlling aim (Berdayes 2002, Glenn 2019: 15–76, Hopper & Macintosh 1998, Rogobete 2015, Schrift 2013, Ziarek 1998, Zuboff 2019).

Another way of discussing the same issue of control, oppression, quantification and the violence of measuring is to read the work and analysis of quantity and machines by Deleuze and Guattari (1983, 1987). Like Foucault, they understand machines, and even more quantification in capitalism as inescapable and a good reason to despair and give up any way of either thinking or connecting to anything that would be social outside the machine (because that 'outside' does not exist in practical terms according to their analysis). For them, the way for humans to escape, or at least to stop being machines in a machine, is to forget any possibility of an equitable, voluntary and non-violent way to relate to anything, whether living creature or inorganic thing.

Although I do not share this despair in terms of what to do, I use the sharp analysis of what capitalist patriarchy wants and continuously attempts to achieve, and how dangerous and violent technologies and quantity can be. Those technologies, tangible and intangible, are used by capital owners who try to, and can, persuade us that everything is lost because we are all living in this same exploitative and oppressive economic and social system. However, what the capitalist side wants or aspires to is not enough to define subjectivities or courses of action for people who belong to another class or a social group that is struggling to survive in capitalist patriarchy (Newton 1998, Sawicki 1987). As a woman in patriarchy and a worker in capitalism, I have enough experience as an oppressed person to know that the argument of living in an oppressive system as the end of the struggle is a way of thinking that the oppressed have no luxury to fall for or buy into. Moreover, the collapse of capitalist measuring approaches in times of climate crisis and of one or multiple pandemics is something that occurred before in previous critical historical moments. However, only certain sections of society – as you may imagine, those at the end of the exploitation line – could really understand how it might work in terms of possibilities of resistance (Adkins 2009, Trejo Mendez 2020).

It is within this context that David Graeber's position in his book *Debt* (2011, in particular 1–10, 43–72, 307–60) takes a very material meaning. Graeber raises the question of the deep links between quantification and violence. He is very careful to show that quantification as violence is of course a major trait of capitalism, but it also exists in other patriarchal economic systems. Debt is a practice that realizes this violence as a tool of oppression, in that respect. The historical account Graeber offers shows clearly how quantification and measuring have been used to facilitate the effectiveness of violent power and value transfer from one social group to another. He also showed how quantification relied on violence in order both to be implemented and to be effective as such, that is, to achieve the wealth accumulation in favour of the oppressors' groups.

The same observations are made by M. Lazzarato (2011) who focuses on the 20th and 21st centuries only and analyses debt in neoliberalism. He underlines the disciplinary and governmental uses of debt on and against the population (particularly the worker classes) and shows how this policy is at the core of neoliberalism.

You may understand why I could not agree more and why these insights concerning quantification and violence are of central significance in this discussion. We have also seen this connection between quantities, measures and violence since the pandemic of Covid-19 erupted. For the people who died or saw their health severely degraded because of the illness, the quantities that were prioritized by policy-makers (such as keeping GDP as high as possible, and the government budgets with as low expenditure as possible) were violence, and very physical indeed.

3.A. Is non-measuring a form of violence?

On the other hand, there are cases where not to measure would be violence. The Covid-19 pandemic is an example for this too: The health degradation not only of those who got Covid-19 and recovered, but also of those who were left without any income and had to cope with absolute poverty and hunger during a pandemic is something that has barely attracted any integrated policy-making attention. Without those quantities, policy-makers get away with leaving the vast majority of the population without any adequate support. Poverty and hunger are very physical and very quantity-related too: when they are inflicted on someone, this person is suffering physically as well, due to the lack of adequate nutrients and adequate quantity of calories, apart from the emotional and mental suffering of not being able to survive in a capitalist economy.

We have other examples as well of activities that require quantification and are very necessary in everyday life, with or without a pandemic. The most common example is preparation of food: cooking needs some quantification of ingredients, energy to be used and time to achieve the preparation of foodstuff. Cooking entails a great deal of quantification in reality, even if in various traditions or recipes, the quantities are not precise, or must not be precise in order for the recipe to be successfully implemented. Without this quantification it is impossible to be able to have access to food and survive, much more to have access to tasty and healthy food. Apart from the recipe, there are other quantities in cooking that need to be respected in order for the activity to fit the ecosystem in which it takes place or the needs of the people who need the food. If the household has five members, cooking for two people is not what adequate food preparation is.

Another example related to food provision is agriculture. If you do not know how much grain seed you need to sow in a field, or when this should be done, or after how much time you should start a new cultivation after the last one, you are going to deplete the soil, lose your harvest, or both. Although precision might not be common in agriculture, in particular the sustainable form, there are practices that need either to be quantified or even to be precise. For example, in one of the schemes related to preservation of traditional seeds and traditional agriculture methods, I was fortunate to be informed that watering the field at specific hours of the day was minimizing the chances of harmful bugs hatching and becoming overpopulated, and thus reducing the risk of their harming the harvest. There is precision agriculture of course, as a new capitalist agricultural know-how and practice that emerged the last years, which is a completely different thing, because it requires industrial inputs and dependence of the farmer to pre-set quantities and technologies that they do not control or decide about.

Medicine is another important field of activity where quantities and especially precise quantities are very much needed to be known and practised in many cases. If you give medicinal substances to a patient without measuring what quantity of the medicinal drug is going to be used by the patient and when and for how long this use is beneficial for the patient, you are probably going to put the patient in big health trouble, if not outright danger. As with all medical activity, medicine is a practice where without quantity, precision and care by the physician to apply the exact procedure that is needed, the medical intervention is an unbound, unsolicited, and unaccountable physical attack to the body of another person (the patient). That is, in medicine, without quantification, precision and metrical/measuring tools, most or all acts become acts of violence against the patient.

Especially with regard to precision: each of the examples can be different. We have seen that some aspects of cooking need to be precise, but in most cases quantification usually does not need to be precise. It is interesting to see that various traditions of food preparation also have different approaches to quantity precision. Imprecision or variable precision approaches allow for adaptation to seasonal and local conditions and for creativity or innovation.

In agriculture, approximation might be allowed or it might be obligatory, depending on weather conditions and other ecosystem features that do not allow a prescriptive, exact quantification. In medicine, quantification might need to be very precise in some cases, and any vagueness of measuring might kill the patient. You cannot just say 'the patient has fever' if you are a health practitioner, because if the patient has a very high fever, they need a different type of treatment than for a fever of 37 °C. One needs to count the fever as precisely as possible and then define the procedures and the quantities linked to it to make sure that the fever is tackled.

It seems that quantification and measurement are in many cases or social frameworks linked to violence – but non-quantification and vagueness might also be linked to violence. Our problem and our quest in this case, therefore, is not quantification as such but violence. We need to be able to track violence and its effects in a quantifying or non-quantifying practice and expose the violence and the quantification (or non-quantification) that sustains it.

What appears therefore to differentiate the cases described by Graeber and the examples of quantified activity described here is the character and aim of each use of quantification. The creatures and social relations that the quantities are supposed to reproduce are very important in order to distinguish whether a practice leads to violence and injustice (Espeland & Stevens 2008).

As a consequence, there is no unidimensional relationship between measurement or quantification with violence. At least, we cannot think of them and their relationship as ahistorical or outside context. We need to examine each measuring practice and each quantity within its social and historical context and decide what their relationship is to oppression and exploitation. We have seen already and we will see in some of the following chapters that violence and measurement can be antithetical. Their connection or antagonism depends on the context of the social relation that is under examination in each situation.

The above position does not mean that a quantification practice has not been designed or created with the intention to exert violence on humans or nature. There are quantities that are inherently violent and they have been created to be so from the very beginning of their use. This is also a matter of context and this is why we need to be careful to examine each practice in its social and historical framework.

In the next chapters we will discuss not only the needs that require quantity approaches to be used but also how those approaches are formulated and in what way they function in an economic activity that aspires to be better than capitalist.

4

Approaches, research methodologies and the quantitative methods problem

Although the book is in reality discussing concepts and ways of understanding economic phenomena that might be useful if anyone wants to learn more or experiment with grassroots or collectively organized economic activity, it draws most of its ideas from field research. I have done that research during various periods, but mostly during the years 2009–2019. The research includes formal projects, for which I was affiliated to a university or research institute, and various informal projects, for which I was not affiliated to any higher education institution and I was doing research as a second work shift, while I was working in other sectors.

I also use any research and any other sources about the topic I can find. However, given that the field of grassroots economic initiatives is under-researched and under-theorized, I need to rely mostly on my research findings.

My approach is and has been oriented towards grounded theory (Charmaz 2006, Glaser & Strauss 2006). I do research usually without having any hypothesis to test or any specific theoretical framework in which I will try to fit my findings. Much less do I research by sticking only to the research questions I had at the beginning of any project. The research starts with investigating the field or the activity as such, and if it is possible to theorize with the data that have been gathered, that is fine. If theory cannot be constructed, that is also fine, in the sense that getting to know how a certain economic phenomenon is taking place is also a finding.

No doubt, I have my own ideological and political background and this I bring with me in all my research, writings and theoretical endeavours. However, my quest with economics is to learn about economic practices that are not capitalist and, if possible, not patriarchal either. Consequently, I have many times started a project with certain assumptions (that I did not recognize at the time as assumptions), which were challenged or shattered as my research was proceeding. And I have proceeded and concluded research projects with more questions that I had at the beginning, but also with additions or modifications of the project, in order to integrate some basic aspects of the economic phenomena that the initial design of the research had missed.

The process of doing research without the strict structure of forming a hypothesis from the very beginning seems, and indeed sometimes is, messy and uncertain. It is even messier when there is no theory from which I start my project, and when the research is ending it is impossible to construct any definitive analytical framework for the activity I am studying. At the same time, this way of doing research allows me to go back to existing theories and previous research while I am collecting data and analysing them. In cases in which it seems that an existing approach can provide useful analytical insights about an economic phenomenon, I use it. In cases in which the research findings do not seem to be easily explained by anything I can find in literature, I try to understand what I have found; and in cases in which it is possible to create an explanation about it (that is, theorize), I do it. In various cases, I might be using more than one theoretical framework in order to explain an economic phenomenon I am interested in.

In general, my approach is that of a learner. I am ready, if not happy, to revise my views or change them, and discard any explanation or theory that does not really help with understanding the economic phenomena I am interested in. I am also very persistent in keeping a theoretical framework that to many, especially economists, might seem irrelevant, if that helps me understand economic activity.

As you may have already seen, I have a strong feminist orientation in my thinking. The second and third chapters stemmed from years of work, research and reflection. The position that patriarchy is an economic system is for the time being the best analytical framework I can use for understanding grassroots economic activity, and it emerged organically through years of research. I mean, I did not have that position when I started my research project as a PhD student in 2009.

Another approach that has greatly affected my thinking but also my methods of researching and theorizing is grassroots economics. This is an approach that Dr Ferda Donmez-Atbasi (University of Ankara) and I have developed through research collaboration since October 2010. The real name of the approach, which in formal terms is a research programme, is Bacılar, which means *sisters from the same mother* in Turkish. We wanted to learn what economic thought and practice people outside academia know and use in their economic activity, and it was not easy to find economic literature that was interested to present this type of knowledge. In this approach, we use any source that is available, not only academic literature and not only economic literature. Everything might contain economic ideas, from everyday practices to social movement activities and discourse, and from folk culture to academic literature in other social sciences, life sciences or environmental sciences.

From the research I have done so far within the framework of Bacılar or grassroots economics, it seems that there is plurality outside the economics departments. Perceptions about nature, value, human effort, gender relations or economic justice are debated and contested everywhere, while we keep formal economic thought confined to neoliberal capitalism as the only economic system to organize or to criticize.

I am all for criticizing capitalism, but I want to go further than that. In reality, grassroots economics as a research programme is a type of grounded theory, but also practice, in the sense that I am a learner and student of the grassroots economic initiatives and their members. If we do not have enough or adequate research and theory about a social clinic, that does not mean that the people who run a social clinic do not know how to run it and do not know its importance. In some cases, they run their own research or learning projects for their own purposes. People in grassroots initiatives are fully aware that what they are doing has important meaning(s) and that those meanings are created through practice and discourse of those same people who work in the initiative.

Therefore, my approach is that I also learn from my research participants but also from the people who in political economic terms wage an important struggle of survival (at least). If no one other than the people who use a parallel currency in Greece knows about how it works, why would I pretend that economic literature (that has no information about that question) knows better?

Learning from my participants and becoming a student of collective endeavours does not mean that I might not have my own ideas and critique about those same activities. As with all teachers, the student can and has to disagree if need be, just like the teacher can disagree and correct the student if something has not been understood well. Grassroots economics as an approach allows this interaction, without erasing the contributions to knowledge of the members of the grassroots schemes.

In practical terms, the research data have been acquired through the use of multiple research methods, like ethnographic-qualitative observation by participation, informal discussions, formal open-question interviews, mapping, questionnaire survey, and discourse/text analysis. The combination of methods in this field has been and still is necessary, first because the field is under-researched; second, because the multiple approaches contribute to a better understanding of the activity; and, finally, because we need triangulation processes in order to do justice to both the participants' hard work but also to the aims they try so hard to serve through their activity. By triangulation I mean the collection of various types of data and the use of various ways of analysing those data, in order to make sure that a supposed finding is not emerging only because of the method of analysis or the form of data one collects. For example, by using mostly quantitative data in economics, especially data in official currency, we end up with a certain perception about the economy that is research-based but obviously does not represent vast parts of economic activity, like the unpaid work that women might be doing at home or in their communities.

There is awareness among economists and experts of other disciplines about the issues they are facing in representing economic (or political economic) activity through quantity, and there is extensive critique within the economics discipline about the use of mathematics in analysis (Berman & Hirschman 2018, Boumans 2005, 2007, Meikle 2000, Mennicken & Nelson Espeland 2019, Porter 1995, Revoy 1998, Velupillai 2005). The problems are not new and in many cases the refinement of methods and approaches stemmed from this critique exactly. However, if one is focused only on capitalist relations of production and distribution, one is trapped in following capitalist understandings of quantity and answering questions that perceive the economy as only and continuously capitalist.

Moreover, I use public internet sources or platforms for research, and the research was conducted in the open, by letting participants know who I am, why I am there and what I am looking for. When any research-relevant information comes to me via the internet outside my research activity, I always let people know that I am interested in the information for research purposes, I ask whether I can file the information and state who I am and how they can find me in case they want to contact me in the future concerning that information they provided.

As I mentioned already, a major problem in my research field (economics) is quantity. Although I often use qualitative methods, my research shows how important quantitative approaches are to understand and investigate the economic phenomena that are linked to non-mainstream modes of transaction and production. There is a whole quantitative world that does not exist in economic textbooks and when a glimpse of it exists in anthropology or other social science writings, it is marginalized as non-economic or, if economic, as non-quantifiable in economic terms (Waring 1999).

Thus, there is a dire need for appropriate quantitative methods. By *appropriate quantitative methods*, I mean methods and approaches of quantitative aspects of the activity under examination that would reflect the realities of the grassroots economic initiatives. The appropriate quantitative methods would also be useful for the communities themselves to have a better picture of their own activity and answer their own questions with or without mediators from academia (Sotiropoulou 2020a).

My research work so far has by conviction followed the path of quantification and measurements that my research participants were using. It would be impossible to understand what they are doing and what economic arrangements they construct if I held as basic perceptions of quantity what mainstream economics or the mainstream economy use as quantity samples and measures.

As a result, I started learning the quantities as 'taught' by the scheme members and I developed practices of counting in many ways and of understanding quantity in various non-mainstream manners. For example, I learned to count the hours an assembly might last; count how many men and how many women participate in a gathering; whether there are any kids and how many of them, whether the kids are just playing around or they work in the initiative (they do light tasks but this is still work in practice) and what they do. I also learned to pay attention to the seasonality of the activities, and to who is doing this work and which social groups they belong to; or how needs are anticipated in an initiative and by which means, how quickly and through which procedures they are provided for.

This book emerged from that quest. It contains all major findings concerning quantity perceptions of the people who participate in grassroots initiatives. It discusses what they measure, how and why, and how they use, if at all, digital technologies to implement those measurements. It is in reality my early attempt to present, if not adequate quantitative methods, at least what up until now is an adequate set of quantitative thought(s) that is both grassroots and collective. Those ways of thinking and acting can possibly give us hints on how to proceed with both perceiving quantities and measures that are not capitalist and, hopefully, not patriarchal. In terms of academic practice, they would be a starting point for finding or creating the adequate quantitative methods we need to analyse this type of economic activity.

Part Two

The practices of quantifying otherwise

My quest with different approaches to quantification and machine use as they emerge from grassroots activity is obviously one that still continues. In the following chapters, I present my findings until now, concerning some main points that are essential for understanding quantity and the activities related to it. I examine first the practices in the initiatives as such. Then I discuss how time is perceived and used, how values emerge in this activity, and what role the information and communication technologies are assigned within this framework. Chapter nine is the one dedicated to an explanation of how the use of machines in this context creates challenges for both their users but also for people who want to learn from that use.

The following chapters have been written with the awareness that the quantification practices and the use of technology are enmeshed in the core of each activity. Therefore, the distinctions made in order to describe the activities and specific examples are presented only for analytical purposes. In reality, the activities are complex processes that intertwine the machines, the technologies that those represent and the quantities that are used in performing this economic activity.

5

Quantities and measures in the non-mainstream field

One common characteristic of the practices we are interested in here is that they take place within the framework of various types of organizations or initiatives, which are not incorporated in any form of legal entity. We are talking about informal organizations and groups or assemblies that are open to participation and that have no official existence according to the local law. Legal entities, like small businesses or cooperatives,[1] or the local municipality, can participate in some initiatives or support the schemes through provision of public spaces or by donating in kind resources that the group might need. They do so without becoming members and without having their donation publicized to avoid being accused of marketing co-option of the initiative.

The same initiatives are also very explicitly against using the official currency, or use it to a minimum, even when an initiative needs donations for continuing its activity, like a social clinic or a social kitchen. When support is needed therefore, donations are requested in kind. Even if some official money is donated in some cases, this is not the major part of the resources contributed to the effort. The donated monetary amount is turned into supplies for the initiative as soon as possible.

When I started my field research in 2009, I thought that this dissociation from the formal or usual ways of acting economically was only a principle-based choice of the people who are involved in the initiatives. Thirteen years later, my opinion is that this is not a choice but a necessity, if the initiative is to survive but also to achieve its aims.

At the beginning, fungibility of monetary amounts seemed a good enough reason for this choice. By *fungibility* I mean mismanagement or use of the money for purposes other than the ones the group or organization has set as eligible. Perhaps avoiding official currency is a good way to avoid severe fungibility-related problems altogether. In many cases, the people who participate in the initiatives are proudly stating that they do not accept monetary donations at all. Apart from that, however, it seems that official currency is a measuring tool that makes people think and act in a certain way, which the grassroots groups want to avoid. They do not avoid it only to show off their 'alternative' character, but because they really need to do things that the official currency does not allow them to do.

This effort, which is as much conscious as it takes, is very evident in the parallel currency schemes. People who create a parallel currency have a critical stance concerning the problems of the mainstream economy and its monetary system. For this reason, they try to use other monetary tools that can be more helpful for their activities and that can be held under the control of the community. The parallel currency is hoped to be used especially for the economic transactions that are needed in a local community that is otherwise short of official money. The parallel currency communities create is usually in digital form. At least in Greece this is the only form that has been used to represent parallel currencies so far. Some currency schemes used a type of check or voucher that were representing the transaction on paper until the digital information about the transaction was added onto the digital platform of the scheme.

The people who use the parallel currency explain that what they need is a tool to count the value of their transactions that cannot be done in official currency (because this does not exist in their pockets or neighbourhood/area and/or is very difficult to acquire). In many cases, they are also explicit in stating how they want to support small producers of their area. They also want to provide access to goods and services for people who have no access to the mainstream market or whose access is limited due to their low income (Sotiropoulou 2012a: 245–76).

In other words, the parallel currency users need quantification in their economic activity and invent a structure where this quantification is possible. The important feature is that this structure does not take, in principle, as a given the measurements that already exist in the capitalist market.

The problems arise, however, since quantification cannot happen in a vacuum. Given that all currency users are also participating in the mainstream economy, they are already familiar with measurements as represented through official money. In many cases, the needs for the facilitation of transactions and for the simplification of measuring of values lead the users to accept without deliberation that the new currency be pegged to the official one, with a nominal parity 1:1. In that way, they use the mainstream market prices as indicative of what the price in parallel currency should be. In part, this is normal, because people know certain values in the mainstream economy and it is much easier to think through them than re-invent what each item's value can be. However, this means that the habitual character of the valuation is not really challenged and the valuations of the mainstream (capitalist patriarchal) market are normalized by the use of the parallel currency and the whole economic activity that this currency represents.

At the same time, there are people in parallel currency schemes who are supporting the free-market argument. According to their views, market prices can reflect the true value of resources and labour, if they are left to fluctuate on their own, without further intervention; and that the prices will stabilize after some time at levels that are convenient for all to transact with those prices. Stated differently, the quantification through (free) market pricing is thought to be inherently effective and just. Following this argument, the only issue the mainstream economy or the currency scheme might have is related to the accounting unit, that is, the currency we use for this quantification. According to this position, the parallel currency is not introduced to change the monetary system or the economic system at all, but just to increase the volume of money that circulates in the economy. If the quantity of money is increased, according to this view, the economy can continue working properly. Therefore, there is a quantity theory of money that proliferates not only among theorists of parallel currencies but also among practitioners and grassroots groups' members.

The contradiction of being critical of the mainstream monetary system and economy while reproducing its very core assumptions in a new monetary structure is something that has not been discussed yet among communities, to the best of my knowledge. What has indeed started to be discussed since 2012 has been the transfer of pricing levels from the mainstream economy to the parallel currency, due to the pegging of parallel currency to the official one.[2] The measuring tool (that is, the parallel currency) started to show its replication of the injustices of the mainstream market because it was thought to be representing the same amount of value as the official currency. It also seemed that producers of goods, especially food producers, remained underpaid within the currency system. The people who sold used industrial goods (like clothes and shoes) were able to command good prices for items they had not produced but which they had acquired in large quantities during the pre-2010 years because of their class position. In that way, the people who could sell used goods were gaining income in parallel currency that was used to buy food stuff at good prices without losing any official currency they had in their pockets, because they could pay for food with non-official currency (Sotiropoulou 2015a).

Under these conditions, the proliferation of initiatives in Greece that avoid monetary tools altogether is easily understood. Apart from parallel currencies, the other types of initiatives (with the exception of one sui generis scheme) avoid official market valuations as much as possible, and official currency as such. To the rest of the initiatives, one should add time banks. Time banks are parallel currencies that use a quantification of work/effort that intentionally equalizes the value of labour among participants. The aim is to avoid the injustices of valuation between different types of work, e.g. a cleaner's work and a physician's diagnosis. Therefore, time banks are parallel currencies that centrally (pre)define values of contributions. The (economic) freedom of participants is linked to their decisions about which type of work they want to contribute and receive but not on how much value they attribute to each person's work.

Actually, the oldest grassroots economic initiatives in the country were two schemes that were straightforward about avoiding official currency quantifications from the very beginning: a time bank in Athens, established in 2005, effective since 2006; and a double exchange network, for traditional seeds exchange and general non-monetary exchange, established in 2002. Parallel currencies run by grassroots communities appeared in the country from 2009 onwards. If we do not include time banks when counting them, the parallel currency schemes remained the minority of initiatives, despite of the publicity they received from national and international mass media.[3]

In other words, most of the activity this book is about is not monetized at all and in this activity the use and measure of official money is deliberately avoided. Even the economic activity within parallel currency schemes that peg their currency to the euro has many elements that reveal contradictions in perceptions of quantity and measures. In several cases, the real activity within the currency scheme reveals the willingness of the people involved to try other ways of measuring and practising value. For example, people assign prices on produce but deliver it with 'generous measures', providing more quantity of the product sold in parallel currency than the original pricing would suggest. Or, along with monetized transactions, many non-monetary exchanges or gift-giving take place in parallel or at the expense of the use of the monetary measure (Gemmill and Mayhew 1995: 81–109, Sotiropoulou 2012a, 2012b, 2016b).

Whether monetary tools are involved in transactions or not, the main fact persists that precision of measuring becomes a very slight priority, if it is not discarded altogether. People exchange goods and services 'in approximation'/«στο περίπου» and they seem to not bother about this lack of precision. Quite the opposite, imprecise or vague assessment of values and other quantities is what they want in their transactions. In many cases, they despise precision, and the quest for it is seen as a sign of meanness and stinginess.

Precision, in other words, is not only unimportant in their economic activity, it is annoying. It is also perceived as offending all parties involved in a transaction, plus the entire initiative and its principles. In reality, it seems that solidarity is understood in a quantitative way as well, that is, that you cannot be solidary if you count every little bit.

People in grassroots initiatives use measures, of course, but those measures emerge only in specific cases and in ways that go well beyond usual measurement in economics. People might count quantity of foodstuff in bags, baskets, bottles, hampers, and quantity of labour in days (or parts of the day, like afternoons) or in hours.

Official measures like kilograms and grammars exist in the transactions, but from some random checks I had made on the field, the measurements in official measures are the least possible quantity a container might contain. People might state that a bag of handmade soap powder is 100 grams of weight, but usually the bag contains more than this amount.[4] Everything is still an approximation, and in several cases they declare that 'there is no correspondence' between quantities and/or values. 'No correspondence' is very common in particular when they make non-monetary exchanges or when the transactions are spread through time (Sotiropoulou 2012b).

Therefore, what in the mainstream economy would be thought of as unequal exchange is, in the non-monetary realm, a very common practice. People seem to value things and labour in completely different ways than what prices in official currency would reveal. This does not mean that there is no possibility for injustices, as we shall see in Part 3 of this book. However, people might not consider it to be an injustice if they take some quantity less in a transaction now while they give something 'valuable' in return.

In some cases, the transaction continues in time, because the involved parties might continue their economic activity. For example, the person who had a low harvest this year might give more quantity of their produce next year; there is no need to put pressure on them to equalize values immediately if this is not possible for them. In that way, the imprecision of the transaction facilitates all parties to transact now and in the future, establishing a long-term economic interaction that precise quantification would not allow.

Moreover, the more an arrangement diverges from the use of accounting units, the more the rule of immediate and/or obligatory return or remuneration fades out. By *immediate* or *obligatory return* or *payback* we mean the rule that demands that what has been offered needs to be remunerated immediately, whether the receiver can practically give anything back or not. The rule is not related to monetary transactions only and it exists in various non-capitalist economies as well.

In capitalist patriarchy, we are trained to think that the immediate and obligatory return of anything offered is the best and fairest thing to do. In practice, this rule creates many problems to people who for any reason might not be able to remunerate immediately, while they might need something that is necessary for their survival. In societies like ours, which are full of hierarchies and exploitative arrangements at the expense of various social groups based on their gender, sexual orientation, race or skin-colour, ethnicity, religion or ability and age, the immediate and obligatory return works against the people who have less privileges or face discrimination in the economy.

As a consequence, the lack of adherence – or at least lack of strict adherence – to the rule of immediate and obligatory return can be understood as a way of allowing people to transact without being squeezed by the transaction itself. In exchange networks this is very evident, especially because people think of themselves as members of a community who have a long-term relationship with each other and with the community.

An example would be the traditional seeds network, which is nation-wide and specializes in the preservation, dissemination and exchange of traditional seeds and local species of domestic animals. For this network, the dissemination of traditional seeds is free (no remuneration required) and the dissemination of local domestic animals is allowed at the cost of breeding, but no remuneration is allowed for the genetic importance/value of the rare species. The same practice is followed by free bazaars, whether permanent, temporary or occasional, physical or online: you give what you want, you take what you want, you may take without giving, you may give without taking (Sotiropoulou 2012a: 81–128, 277–92).

That does not mean that there are no rules in these 'no obligatory reciprocity' situations. This is where quantities re-enter into the economic activity, but in a completely different way.

For example: when the people package the traditional seeds to be distributed for free in the annual fair of an exchange network that specializes in protection of traditional seeds, they use a certain (small) size of paper envelope/bag, and not a large number of seeds are put in each envelope. Precision does not exist, but the idea is that the thousands of visitors will all have a better chance of acquiring some of the traditional seeds, rather than some getting many, and many getting none. So 'few' is the quantitative rule for each package, and 'many' is the quantitative rule for the number of people who it is hoped will have access to the seeds.

Moreover, in order to support farmers and people who already cultivate in traditional modes and contribute the traditional seeds themselves, the annual fair organizers allow the following arrangement: the exchange between the (professional and amateur) farmers takes place in a designated separate space, before the general sharing takes place. So, the 'inside/farmer–outside/nonfarmer' criterion creates another quantitative distinction among the 'few' and the 'many', just like the timing 'before–after' ensures that farmers have access to the quantity of seeds they need. At the same time, the visitors (who might become farmers in the future or not) are educated that whoever has already invested time and resources in traditional cultivation and preservation of traditional seeds receives 'more' support than people who have not invested the same 'big amount' of effort and resources.

Rules of similar character exist in free bazaars and online free-exchange networks. In some of them, although anyone can take without giving in some instances, the behaviour is discreetly monitored and 'going with empty hands' is not considered to be a good practice, especially if it is a repetitive stance of a participant.

Some bazaars, especially the occasional and regular ones, which do not have any permanent space to keep the shared stuff stored and/or available to the public, impose limits on how many items one can take each time, or how many and what type of items one can bring each time. The aim is to avoid free-riding on the initiative for very individual purposes, such as sweeping all items or dumping one's warehouse content onto the community. By *free-riding*, we mean that some people might benefit from a collective effort without themselves contributing to that effort in a similar manner or in some way that balances, more or less, the benefit they obtain from the collective activity.

Nevertheless, in many cases, even these rules are bent if need be. A relocation might give freedom to the newcomer to take as many items as they might need. A person who has many kids/dependents at home is allowed to take more items without people even being allowed to comment (to avoid stigmatization). People who might be complete newcomers and might not even speak the local language are silently (but smilingly) directed to the space with offered items. There, they are allowed to take what they need without further ado, whether they take stuff for themselves, their families or friends, who might not be able to visit the bazaar or become members of the network. What is not allowed is to take freely given things and sell them for money (something that is easily traceable in online networks, and the group coordinators are very strict when such a case arises).

6

The question of time

One of the most important quantities or things that are perceived through quantitative concepts is time. There is a huge question whether time should be a quantitative measure and how we can live with time that is not quantitative. We have already seen in chapter three that labour time, in particular the socially necessary labour time, is a contested quantitative measure. The other question is how, if time is experienced as quantity in a certain context, this quantity is perceived and practised.

In the grassroots initiatives in Greece, time is perceived more or less as a quantity, but the perceptions are variable and very different to how the official time measuring in the economy develops. People use the same calendars and clocks as everyone else, but the use of the information coming from those calendars and clocks is different. My research did not focus on the calendar or/and time aspects of the activity, and I therefore have no clear picture whether in some production processes calendars other than the solar one are used. Farmers, in particular those who practise traditional agriculture, tend to use lunar calendars or other traditional time-understanding practices that differ from the official calendar. This is related to natural cycles that farmers need to adapt to in order to improve their harvest and avoid depletion of soil. However, I cannot know the extent to which those time perception practices are employed for agriculture by people who participate in various grassroots initiatives. This would be a fascinating research question for a future project.

However, my findings show that there is extensive adaptation to seasonal changes and annual cycles anyway. The availability of products along with the availability of labour and the availability of everyone's time to participate in a grassroots initiative depend very much on those cycles. Those are natural (or perceived as natural) cycles, of humans and nature. Even when someone is not offering agricultural products through a grassroots initiative, they might be involved with helping others or working for a wage in order to harvest agricultural products that are ready for the mainstream market. In that sense, time has a cyclical character anyway.

It seems, though, that the activities we are discussing here are very much into that cyclicality but also into discussing time as a part of production and distribution processes as well.

In all cases, time is a main tool to organize activities. Every initiative, irrespective of its character, requires a lot of effort and coordination to be realized. Even those events that are organized as one-off arrangements, like an occasional free bazaar in a neighbourhood, require perceptions of time for the people to be able to attend, and also a lot of effort. Effort is very often understood as 'time' to be contributed to the team, by the organizers and other participants of the event.

In the case of time banks, time is the accounting unit by which contributions are measured and valued and understood. Time banks, as mentioned before, are schemes where people use time in order to measure how much effort one has contributed to others. In a time bank, any type of work or labour that is performed in one hour is accounted and/or valued similarly to any other type of work or labour that can be performed in the same time period (one hour).

Time banks are an example of how many questions we (should) have concerning the use of time in our production and sharing practices. A question that people raise, especially when they discuss what type of organization or initiative they want to create, is whether the value of one hour of cleaning is equal to the value of one hour of teaching, and to the value of one hour of healthcare.

In a discussion of an assembly taking place in 2009 in a small city in Greece, I saw people discussing this exactly. There were those who were saying that for reasons of equality and justice, one of hour of any type of work should be equally valuable to one hour of any other type of work. Time banks are based on the idea that all humans have the same 24 hours to live each day, which means that each person's 24 hours should have the same value as the 24 hours of any other person. Moreover, a lot of work is undervalued in the economy and many people want to give a chance to elevate the estimation and practical value of labour types that are not appreciated enough. This is particularly important for reproduction work, like domestic work, that goes unpaid or un-remunerated or underpaid in capitalism.

There were of course other people who at the same assembly were discussing whether it is fair to equalize the value of different types of labour like this; because, they said, some people spend time before being able to offer their services, in order to receive the education and training required for them to be qualified for the job. Medicine, that is, physicians, is an example brought forward in this case: in Greece they spend many years (ten or more) in order to be fully qualified, and this time needs to be somehow remunerated, according to that position.

Nevertheless, this discussion about the time invested in each type of labour is not quite developed. In a sense, the time is perceived without its class or gender or even ethnicity repercussions. In a society where studying medicine is not only a matter of time or personal willingness to study, but also a matter of having the resources and/or privileges necessary for one to be able to study for ten years, seeing time as something unrelated to those privileges creates an unclear picture of what time is. Therefore, many people who could have been great doctors might just be factory workers because that was the only feasible option they had to survive. And many people who have been great doctors, were able to become so because other people had to spend time in the fields and factories to prepare the food and clothes and medical equipment that the doctors need to get trained and then become fully able to provide their services. Even if an individual never wanted to spend ten years as a student of medicine, they still produce other things that the doctors need to use in order to be doctors (Schumacher 2011).

We need to recognize that time banks try to do this exactly, that is, acknowledge the time spent by all participants within the scheme and in their activities previous to the time bank. The appreciation of the importance of all types of labour through time is a way to see expertise in what the mainstream economy labels 'unskilled' work. It is also a way to redistribute value of labour from those whose expertise and previous work is recognized by capitalism to those whose expertise and work is not recognized and valued by the same economic system.

However, even if we perceive time as an accounting unit that delivers labour equality or value equality within a time bank scheme, there are many issues of time-accounting that are open. For example, time banks cannot integrate into the accounting the use of other inputs such as use of raw materials, energy or machines. In that way, the labour can be counted in human hours, but the work done by nature either as raw materials, or primary materials or as energy, cannot be accounted. Human labour is not a substitute for natural resources anyway, but only to a certain, rather limited extent. On the other hand, the redistribution or equality explored through the time hours assigned to human effort, reveals this in a clear way.

Time banks create a contrast to the perceptions of values based on labour time needed to be spent to extract a raw material from earth: one thing is the labour time needed for the extraction; another thing is, for example, the mineral that is extracted, which cannot be created by human labour. I mean, the mineral cannot be regenerated in the place from where it has been extracted. Neither can any amount of human labour restore the ecosystem that was affected or even destroyed because of that human labour that was needed to extract the mineral. Therefore, when people enter a time bank and start transacting with each other, they really expose the difference between human labour and other inputs needed for production. The inability to account with time for the value of natural resources is inherent in time-accounting of value. Yet, capitalist patriarchy seems to pretend it does not exist, by assigning the value of zero to natural resources and seeing them only through the lens of human time (labour) needed to extract them and process them.

Even if we put the issue of natural resources used in production aside, there are other issues related to the use of time as accounting unit of human effort and its value. A major question has been how to handle the time units when a teacher is teaching or training a group of, let's say, five people. The teacher may work for just one hour, but the five students are 'indebted' for an hour each. What happens with the four hours that are obviously in excess if one uses hours as accounting units? The four hours need to be accounted in such a way so that they are not lost, but also used in ways that treats all scheme participants fairly.

A solution would be to pay the teacher with more hours than one. This, however, would break the basic valuation rule of the scheme, that one hour of work of any type equals one hour of work of any type. Another solution would be to use some of the excess hours to fund the community as such, so that they are able to hire services for an event organizing or for further education dissemination. This solution, chosen by some schemes, seems to be holding the one hour equals one hour rule, but at the same time, it makes the teacher an obligatory donor irrespective of their class position. Moreover, the one hour of work as the only measure of value does not take into account the intensity of work of teaching five people instead of one, for example.

These are issues that have not been resolved yet but they are made visible in time banks and in the discussion about time as accounting unit. Those same issues exist in capitalist economy but they are not paid attention to. Those who can command better prices for their services, that is, those who can enforce recognition of the value of their work in the market, can negotiate issues of labour intensity or issues of environmental protection and sustainable natural resource management. Those who cannot negotiate values because class and other inequalities define both their time and their produce as less valuable than those of other people, are 'price takers'. The time-value issues in their case are made invisible, and only when time is used in a more egalitarian way are the issues exposed.

When time is not used as an accounting unit, it is more broadly employed as a very important tool in order to facilitate sharing and transactions between people who might have different access to means of production and different needs throughout a calendar year or their life cycle. Seasonality of production and seasonality of income availabilities may cause people to face either hardship or even simple inability to perform a transaction or/and improve their lives.

The lack of precision in transactions is often accompanied with extension of the transaction activities over time. An agreement can be, for example, that 'you give me tomatoes/olive oil/cheese/soap whenever you can/have or after your next harvest'. The understanding that people do not transact in one-off situations because they cannot or because it is not the season for the product one wants, allows for spreading or decentralizing over time of many economic activities that the usual (academic) understanding of barter does not include or does not take into account.

The perception of barter as immediate return or remuneration activity does not represent what non-monetary transactions are about. There is always, of course, the instantaneous transaction case, where people exchange at the same time both of their offers. But there are many other cases, where immediacy is not preferred and delay in remuneration is agreed or expected. People in hardship or in sectors where seasonality is very important are allowed to transact at the pace that their activity allows, without their contribution been seen as less or delayed as the usual perception of barter or payment in the mainstream market is understood.

In some cases, it might not be hardship that brings this time-accounting of the transaction, but also the quest for a better life as such. For example, the best olive oil, the freshly made one, is available in winter. If one insists on receiving immediate payment in September, one is going to receive last winter's olive oil, even if the other party has every good intention of providing the best olive oil available. In the mainstream economy, such arrangement is seen as pre-payment in official currency. In economies where immediate remuneration is not necessary, the perception of immediate–non-immediate does not exist, or at least does not affect the value of the transactions. Fresh olive oil is always available in winter and whoever produces it, along with whomever wants to have some, needs to abide with this seasonality one way or another.

Time is also used as a measuring tool in collective production and sharing. For example, in collective cultivations members might have their own plots (not really property but just shared field space for cultivation) and the communal ones to take care of. The collective members usually arrange that each member will take care of the field for one day, taking care too for the field parts where the other members of the initiative have their separate plots of land. In that manner, labour and time spent on the activity are shared in ways that minimize effort and management-monitoring costs for everyone. As a result, people might have (small) produce with minimum effort and pressure because time is perceived as collective in a production setting that is also collective.

The same happens in solidarity initiatives. Solidarity workers arrange shifts in order to work for a social clinic or a social kitchen. By solidarity workers I mean the people who contribute with their personal effort to the grassroots initiative that aspires to provide the community with a good that is both produced and distributed collectively and without any formal payment or remuneration. Therefore, the solidarity workers, even if they are not paid (and perhaps because they are not paid in a capitalist patriarchy but still want to work collectively), have a quite sophisticated time schedule in order to be able to perform the tasks that are needed for their initiative. The time they spend can be production in an individual manner, like a person who takes food to cook at home for a social kitchen; or in a collective manner, like the people who distribute the food or the health workers who provide healthcare in a social clinic. Participation in discussions and assemblies is also collective work but is not accounted as work in the shifts, although people recognize the time-toll that assemblies take in order for the group to coordinate their activities.

The perception of time as something that can be used to allow people to contribute when they can is fundamental in collective arrangements, especially in solidarity initiatives. Many people who might have received solidarity for a period of time without being able to contribute become involved in production when they feel they can contribute. This might happen after months or years but it is very common, that is, to see people who benefited from an initiative to continue participating in it as contributors.

There are of course various questions of concentration of offers during some times of the year, overwork in other times, solidarity for solidarity workers and the handling of time schedules of the entire group (Sotiropoulou 2016a). There are occasions when the group needs more people to get involved and occasions when the contributions are many and the members can have a very light schedule. The basic idea is that the amount of labour needed is such that time will allow people to reciprocate on their own will and when they are able to help. Variations in people's lives and people's life cycles, seasonality of production and seasonality of employment and income available are issues that we need to keep always in mind. Those same seasonalities and activity cycles can turn into a facilitating or problematic factor depending on the economic arrangement a person is involved in. The grassroots initiatives create other times or types of time that can work together with seasonalities along with changes in each person's or group's needs, by allowing flexibility to the greatest extent possible. At least, this is their aim, even if it is not always achieved.

7

The question of value

We saw in the previous chapter how time is used to equalize values of labour and how time is manipulated so that people can participate in the transaction without being squeezed because they cannot reciprocate immediately.

We also saw the deliberate effort in various cases to support or enhance the value of labour that in the mainstream economy is undervalued. In those arrangements, the healthcare provider who is unpaid or underpaid in the mainstream economy is accepted to have provided labour of equal value to the value of labour provided by the physician. The measuring of value therefore shifts from measuring something that can differ from one worker to another (the specificities of each person's labour) to something that is similar for everyone, that is, how much time one spends on the activity they offer.

In the mainstream, capitalist patriarchal economy, a similar – at least superficially – arrangement is accepted. We have seen in chapter three that the socially necessary labour needed to produce anything, like a physician's advice, is the only measure of the value of labour. At least, this is what capitalism aspires to or declares as practice. We have seen in the previous chapter that in the discussions about time banks, some people brought forward the question of how we can account for the time a physician has spent in order to be educated to provide medical services. We also saw that the intensity of labour is not accounted for in a time bank.

Capitalism aspires to account for all those problems with time. The arrangement is based on the assumption that all time spent by a person to be able to provide any type of labour must be accounted in the value of their labour. Actually, it is not 'all time' but the socially necessary time, that is, an abstract anticipation of how much time any average worker needs to produce a specific good or service given the technology and means of production available to them. Of course, there is no average worker in reality, and capitalism claims that as a system it can account for the uniqueness of worker's effort. Therefore, capitalism states that the capitalists reward productivity as well, that is, the abilities, velocity, smartness and experience of each worker, something that the time banks intentionally do not do. We have seen in the previous chapters that capitalism in reality differentiates values of labour according to hierarchies that are not relevant to the task that the time or money measures but to the social position and privileges of the person who works.

In terms of discourse, however, it is the time banks that appear to equalize unequal values. Yet, as we have also seen in the previous chapter, time as measure is not so good at reflecting values in general. Or, time might be a good tool, at least for human labour, under certain conditions, but it seems that capitalist patriarchy does not see the time of everyone. According to the exploitative and hierarchical system that capitalism is, it only recognizes the time spent by certain groups of people, who by sheer coincidence always happen to be those who have social and economic privileges.

Therefore, if we want to be really using time to account for people's contributions to the economy, we have to account for the time spent by everyone and not only by the physician who gives advice to a patient. It has already been mentioned that the physician could have the time and privilege to study for many years and continue their studies and specialization in medicine, because other people were producing food, clothes, houses and medical equipment for the physician. Those people's time was spent on types of labour that capitalist patriarchy does not value as equal to the physician's expertise, although they are absolutely necessary for the physician's expertise to be produced.

In practice, we would have no medical expertise concentrated in one person who can quickly give accurate advice and operate on a patient in a critical condition before the patient loses their lives, if all those people did not spend time for years doing other non-medical labour, so that the physician could become the expert they are in the surgery. The value of the physician's labour therefore consists not only of the physician's personal labour, effort, abilities and dedication to save lives, but also of the labour of many other people, who might be working in the same clinic with the physician (and without their labour the physician cannot perform any medical act), but who also were working in fields far away from the physician's location to produce food for them or other items they might need. It takes a society or a planet to create a physician in an ER room, but for the reasons we have already explained, capitalist patriarchy accounts only for the time of the labour of the physician and not of the other people who worked for or with them.

What is important is that in a time bank, but also in other initiatives of collective production like social clinics and social kitchens, this unfair perception of valuing only certain types of labour is deliberately resisted. Whether the groups succeed in reducing this inequality of value measuring is another discussion for a later chapter. The important thing is that if a community accepts that all people's labour is important for everyone else, and that without it the prestigious labour cannot be realized, value becomes a collective creation that cannot be individualized. What the physician offers to the community is a community achievement as much as it is an individual success of a person who struggled to learn complicated processes related to health and healthcare.

In the same way, labour that is not valued at all in the mainstream economy, because it is provided in spaces that are not monetized, is very much needed for the economy. The most common example is domestic and care labour, labour that is done in the private spaces of homes where people have to eat, sleep, get clean, and recreate themselves. This labour is mostly done for 'free', in the sense that it is not paid nor even recognized as labour (with everything that means about income, access to healthcare, accident insurance, rights to pension, rights to unionize). Another example is community labour that is also done for 'free', that is, at the workers' expense, in order for communities to cover their needs and reproduce themselves. In all those cases, we see labour that is done without being accounted in any way, not even as time spent, which would have been the simplest way to account for it. Despite the importance of domestic and care labour and of labour done by communities, this is not in any way understood by capitalist patriarchy as part of the value of the labour of a physician or any other person whose work is highly valued in the mainstream economy.

Time banks as structures seem to have a better understanding of the complexity of labour value, although obviously time-accounting is not a panacea and has its own complications when used, as we saw in the previous chapter. Measuring labour time as equal for everyone is a way not only to equalize value but also to recognize that everyone owes to everyone else and that it is impossible to individualize values, especially when we are talking about human effort. By saying that one hour of cleaning equals one hour of physician expertise the group recognizes that the cleaner has contributed to the physician's expertise as much as medical advice contributes to the cleaner's well-being. In other words, time banks or people who think that we must re-evaluate cleaning labour are doing this not as a favour or concession to the cleaner but as an obligation to recognize the interconnectivity of values in an economy.

However, time bank members were recognizing the complexity of other types of labour. For example, the production of food in the field cannot be accounted properly not only because of the inputs or contributions by nature to the foodstuff offered to the community but also because of the nature of the work. For example, for someone to have access to one bag of tomatoes, the time spent by the farmer to offer this might be minimal. This is the case because farming is already an activity of scale: fruits, vegetables and dairy are produced on a large scale even if the farm is traditional, small-scale, sustainability-oriented and does not use any industrial methods. There are some proposals (though not in Greece) for accounting time by minutes, but even their proponents are not sure whether they would be handy, or whether people would like to enter a by-the-minute accounting mode when they so much avoid precision when accounting their contributions.

On an individual level, therefore, the farmer's work, agriculture, cannot be accounted through time as easily as other types of work. On a collective level the importance of the farmer's work and the hours spent in the fields and in the farm are extensive, and often beyond the usual office hours that a physician spends working. Farmers might have to work more than 8 hours per day in times of harvest, under very harsh weather conditions in order to produce large quantities of food that for each individual might represent a tiny part of the farmer's time but a huge part of the consumer's ability to survive. These disparities have not been resolved in systems like time banks. Yet, we have to admit that the debate that time banks raise makes these questions much more visible than what is shown by the mainstream market and their prices.

The complexity of valuing is a huge topic to which a short chapter cannot do justice. What is necessary to mention here is how this complexity is reflected in the variety of grassroots schemes. The variety of grassroots economic organizing reflects, among other things, not only the variety of needs to be covered, but also the different types of economic values and the variety of the processes of valuation in the economy. This is crucial, because for capitalism, as we have explained previously, the value tends or is aspired to be constituted in one way only, while its expression is acceptable only in monetary terms, and even then, mostly in official currency. In all those grassroots initiatives, however, value is not 'a thing', much less a unique process that is used in all cases for all transactions. The variability of valuation processes is the central characteristic in this type of economic activity and we have given various examples concerning equalization of labour values or long-term exchanges that keep the value of seasonal production high instead of pressing or squeezing a farmer without a harvest to pay another person back immediately with meagre means of remuneration.

The other characteristic that stems from that variability is that values are explored in many ways. The needs of the people participating in a grassroots initiative and of the group as a whole are usually the criteria for arranging an initiative in a certain way. Those same criteria are also used for choosing to create values in certain ways.

This can explain preliminarily why the monetization of the activities is relatively reduced. Even if we count the time banks as currency schemes, parallel currencies are not as common as one might expect. The variability of needs that people want to satisfy through the use of grassroots economic initiatives can also explain the variability of rules, along with the flexibility of those rules in the initiatives. In other words, political economic principles are considered to be important for organizing a grassroots arrangement or transaction, even if the aims of the principles are not always realized in practice.

In some cases, measuring is not allowed and the literal price of what is offered is zero. A very telling example is the sharing of traditional seeds for free, that is, without reward. Another example is the sharing of food or health care or education in social kitchens, social clinics or social institutes, where people who provide their labour are not paid or remunerated and the services are available for free to people who might need food, healthcare or education. The assignment of zero price to traditional seeds or to shared food or healthcare is linked to a completely different value than the one the monetary economy assigns. If we are talking about the capitalist patriarchal economy, then the absence of a price leads to devaluation of anything the value of which is not expressed in monetary terms.

Therefore, when people in grassroots initiatives do not want to measure value and to declare this, they assign a price of zero, they do this in order to state more or less that the value cannot be measured. The decision that the value of something cannot be measured directly affects the way that the activity takes place. We have already seen that in the sharing and exchange of traditional seeds, the farmers, that is, the people who have already contributed to the preservation of traditional varieties, have priority. At the same time, the people who have not contributed to the preservation of the traditional varieties can also access the seeds for free, and they are asked to cultivate and share them for free, in the same way they acquired the seeds. That means, the activity as such and the valuables that are assigned a zero price reach the members of the initiatives and/or the members of the local community in certain ways influenced by the decision of non-measuring and by the perception of values that can be priceless and absolutely necessary at the same time (Daskalaki et al. 2018, Sotiropoulou 2016b).

From the above, it seems that economic activity can be carried out very well without precision and without accounting units at all. Important economic activities like the preservation of traditional seeds or the provision of healthcare can be performed without measuring values. Transactions without immediate or obligatory reciprocity can take place in various occasions and in order to cover a range of needs, and people can still be happy with those transactions and continue to pursue them.

The mainstream assumption or stereotype, however, that we have in economics is exactly the opposite. The assumption is that non-monetary economic activity is not handy; it is assumed that non-monetary transactions or pluri-monetary transactions are neither easy nor efficient. It is also assumed that people will proceed to an economic activity without using official currency only if they lack the latter and that they will return to money, especially the official one, when they have access to it (Sotiropoulou 2012b).

Yes, of course, in several cases people might be using official currency as well in their economic life and they might start using other transaction modes if the official currency is short in the economy. However, the lack of official currency in the market at some point of time does not explain why people would turn to other currencies or transaction modes without money, instead of trying to affect the monetary situation in other ways, even with political lobbying. It does not explain either why people might choose a certain structure for a non-monetary arrangement or for a parallel currency scheme. Why do people who might not have enough official currency choose to hold a social clinic instead of a parallel currency? Why would they bother to have a free bazaar instead of selling second-hand items?

The point is encapsulated by an account I received from a research participant several years ago. He was, in his view, reasonably well-off.

He had been involved with grassroots initiatives, sharing access to his land and working as much as everyone else to cultivate collectively in traditional modes. The explanation he gave was that all his money was not enough to guarantee that his children have access to organic, that is, chemical/pesticide-free food. The quantifications the official currency and capitalist market created, although seemingly to his benefit, were not able to measure the value of the food he needed for his family.

Those same quantifications are much less able to create the economic conditions necessary to produce the food he needed to acquire. He stated that even the certifications of the organic products were not enough for him. He wanted to know how the food is produced. He preferred to start working collectively together with other people who shared his ideals of sustainable agriculture and healthy food rather than paying premium prices to strangers. He also contributed land for collective use to the group. The people involved in the collective cultivation projects were working together and sharing the produce among themselves. That involved other measuring practices where people had to share the workload and the harvest afterwards. Therefore, even someone who had access to official currency had to be involved with other collective measuring practices that were ensuring food safety throughout the production process for that person to have the economic outcome he wanted to have.

Finally, one more point concerning value: this book does not aspire to discuss theories of value as such, and it would go beyond the scope of this analysis to discuss perception and production of value(s) in grassroots initiatives. As you may see, from the examples we have seen so far, the existing theories of value are not a very good fit to explain the grassroots economic activity as such, and they are also questioned by the examples we will see in the next chapters. This is normal, given that the theories of value refer to capitalist systems and, depending on the use of them, they might have a satisfactory explanatory power for those systems.

I have discussed issues of value in the past (Daskalaki et al. 2018, Sotiropoulou 2016b) and I would need another book to write about value approaches that are more appropriate to understand the value issues in the activity we are interested in. The important point, however, is that the whole effort performed by grassroots initiatives concerning the perceptions and use of quantities, measures and technologies is a form of management labour that is fundamental in organizing the economic activity they want to have. Without this labour those activities would not exist, nor would they raise such important questions of practice and theory. I share the view that management work is labour that produces value (Cheng et al. 2019: 173–219, 251–80, Lau 2020). The questions related to it refer to what type of value this is, which economic system it reproduces, and in what way. Stated differently: without this organizing and managing work, we would have no possibility of seeing different valuations, measures, quantities, technology uses and productive results materializing in the economy, much less would we be able to discuss them in a book.

Information and communication technologies (ICTs) in the non-mainstream field

All grassroots economic initiatives use ICTs one way or another. In various cases the use might be limited in volume or limited to the use of a certain technology only. In other cases, the use of ICTs is extensive because the whole activity has been constructed to take place mainly through internet. There are cases where people might not use ICTs at all or they use them to a very marginal extent, but those are very rare and they are usually not directly related to the groups and initiatives I have investigated, that is, they might be associated to a member of a group but not directly members of it. Because I was focusing on more or less organized group activities, my research has not included un- or disorganized economic activity that takes place without the use of ICTs, but through the use of other communication and information knowhow, such as customary practices.

From what my research participants have told me, and also from what sparse references in written sources mention, it seems complex non-monetary or semi-monetary transactions never stopped taking place in Greece. In other words, before the dissemination of mobile phones and the internet, people were doing similar things in that same economy, even if academic research omitted to document their activity in previous decades. Therefore, the question about other ways of organizing and coordinating non-mainstream transaction modes and the history of this activity remains, and it would need to be addressed with another research project.

A main feature of this type of contemporary grassroots economic activity is the way by which people use information and communication technologies and platforms, along with low-technology tools. By *low-technology tools* we mean technologies that are considered to be low-technology in a certain contemporary context, without really accepting the hierarchy that the terms of 'high' and 'low' imply in discourse. In reality there are no 'low' technologies, in the sense that technologies we humans use, such as fire, the wheel, cooking or agricultural practices, are definitely 'high' in terms of importance in covering our needs and in terms of skills needed to use them.

In the same pathway of thought, what is considered to be 'high' technology is just one part of various other technologies and know-how that have been created throughout the years: writing is a technology that takes other roles when it is done on the internet or in digital format. Without writing as such, digital information technologies would not have been possible, or even if they were, they would not have the impact they have now. Therefore, the technology that we use today to perform a transaction is one thing, and the transaction mode itself as a technology and know-how is another.

This is of fundamental importance because in some cases, there emerges the impression that parallel currencies or non-monetary economic activity has been caused or promoted by digital technologies that became widely available from the mid-1980s onwards. Nothing could be further from the historical actuality. For example, virtual currencies and non-monetary agreements have been very common in the Mediterranean since at least the Middle Ages, or from the 12th century onwards. Non-monetary transactions appear to have an even longer history than that, although the evidence we have about them is not as systematic as we would like it to be.

This does not mean that the technologies we use in our economic activity do not affect the economic activity as such, or that the technologies do not make a certain type of transaction easier or more difficult in certain contexts. What it means is that we need to place the use of ICTs within their historical material context. We also need to avoid simplistic linear causality connections between the activity we discuss in this book and the existence of those technologies that became widely available the last three decades.

One reason is that those technologies did not become as widely available as we like to think of them. They are well linked to class privileges that require a certain level of individual and collective income or wealth in order for those technologies to be accessible to the majority of the population. Therefore, in a country or region where the private telecommunication companies do not find it profitable to invest in good quality reliable mobile phone services and/or internet networks, even the wealthiest of the locals cannot really have adequate access to those technologies, let alone to be able to coordinate themselves with the other people living in that region.

The other reason is that the under-researched character of this type of economic activity does not allow us to create narratives that conflate the visibility of the activity in the last decades with the existence of the activity. Indeed, the visibility of the activity can probably be well connected to the use of the digital ICTs. However, assuming that what was not visible thirty years ago did not exist does not help to understand the role of ICT in parallel currency use and in non-monetary initiatives today. It does not even help us understand the choices by the people who use ICTs today in their grassroots economic activity.

A major finding is that people use all types of technologies and know-how in order to communicate with others in their group and outside their group and also in order to facilitate the economic activity as such. For example, they use posters in the streets and in the city spaces in order to announce assemblies, the establishment of a new initiative or events related to the economic activity they want to create or support, like a market or a festival. The posters or other material like leaflets are also designed and printed with digital tools. In other words, what seems to be 'low-tech' is quite high-tech in reality. It just takes a very common form, like a paper poster pinned on a news board.

People are also using social technologies and know-how of information sharing. Word of mouth is the most common in small places or among people who know each other due to various other collective activities, like neighbourhood events or social movement organizing. Assemblies are also very common both in the process of establishing a grassroots initiative and in the period after it has been established and needs to be managed. Grassroots decision-making techniques are employed in various ways, which means that in many cases live discussions and gatherings are preferred to the use of digital communication. Those who cannot attend are learning the news or sending their views and opinions through those who can attend a live meeting. In reality, live communication is prevailing over any other way of sharing news or deliberating over an issue.

All those social technologies of collective organizing and management existed before digital ICTs and seem to be able to exist with some independence from them. The Covid-19 pandemic has raised many questions about how this can be affected and whether the digital technologies can facilitate the assemblies that were taking place live before March 2020. The important thing is, however, that the assembly is the way to share information and that live discussion is the preferred way to hold the assembly, although circumstances might not allow or might demand a digital or hybrid (some people meet live, some people join online) gathering.

Some of the grassroots initiatives have (had) their own websites or blogs. Most initiatives' sites were/are in Greek only, because they are meant to be used by their members and not for publicity in general. Even after the surge of interest by local, national and international media about grassroots initiatives in Greece, most of the websites remained in Greek only. This is not weird, because updating the sites and translating them is a quite time-consuming task and all those initiatives are run by people who have to survive economically in the mainstream economy as well, and have to find time to get involved with the grassroots initiative. The latter means that they already give much of their spare time to the community. Given that all those groups are very practice- and task-oriented, the websites are not regularly updated and an English or any other language version of the website is a burden for the people of the group that can be undertaken only in very few cases. Translations in various languages are used to facilitate communication with the community, therefore one might see leaflets or posters in other languages than Greek, but this is not as much the case on the websites.

However, most initiatives use the internet without having their own website or blog. In many cases, they have their own groups or pages on social media, like Facebook and/or Twitter, apart from their website or irrespective of whether they have a website at all. This allows (allowed) them to be easier to find on the internet and be contacted by people in their region or by people who want to communicate with them for any reason. In several cases, the initiatives use blogs and websites of other social movements when they want to make announcements or ask for support. In that case, the texts and information material are prepared by the group who wants to make an announcement and they are just uploaded and disseminated by the other groups and the users of their page.

Some initiatives, especially those who run a parallel currency, use specialized software to facilitate digital registration of each transaction but also cooperation and coordination of their members. Software might range from usual spreadsheets to open-source platforms for parallel currencies that have been developed and made available during the last decades worldwide. In the Greek parallel currency schemes both open source and privately created software was used initially, but as time went by the schemes seem to have turned to open source software. The specialized software platforms allow spaces for discussion (fora) and showcasing the goods that are available in the group. Discussion can take place through emails or through secret/private groups in social media, if the initiative has no website or platform of their own.

The use of specialized software does not preclude the use of generic platforms, social media and technologies such as mobile phones. All available technologies are used in such cases, depending on what need exists and how comfortable people feel with each technology. Therefore, the initiatives show great flexibility concerning what technology will be used in each case, and they usually assign members to help other members learn the required technological tools and/or do the digital tasks that are required by the group to achieve its activity aims. The same policy concerning assistance exists if some group members have no regular access to internet or feel uncomfortable even to use a certain tool or platform.

In general, people involved in the economic activity described in the previous sections are very good and creative in using cable and mobile phones, and much more the internet and the information sources, including electronic mail, and of course social media. The use of social media, especially Facebook, is very common. The option to create a secret group for internal discussions and an open forum on Facebook allows groups to run their activity and at the same time interact with outsiders that want to learn more about it.

I have participated as a researcher in such groups and I have to say that the use of social media for grassroots economic organizing has been a revelation for me. Actually, my research participants were those who persuaded me to start using social media for my research in 2009, although at the beginning I was very reluctant and I shared my reservations with them. They were using Facebook extensively at that time, and for many years to come. Several members of the initiatives were not so favourable to social media (so my participants were very understanding towards me in that respect). For those members, other arrangements of communication were adopted so that they are not excluded form learning the news or from knowing what debates are taking place in the group. The initiatives' members explained to me (and they were right) that I have to learn not only to use those tools because I am a researcher in this field of grassroots economic activity; but also because I had to see how they were using those digital tools for the activity I was studying (and they were right once more).

The use of social media, therefore, by the grassroots economic schemes is as variable as it is in other cases. People adapt the tools to their needs rather than the other way around. From 2009 to 2014, when I had a Facebook research account, I could see how effective they were in using the platform for their purposes and also how quickly they could disseminate news if there was such need. That they knew me and my account (never anonymous, always explaining who I am and what the purpose of the account is) helped a lot, even after the end of my PhD, for them to find me and send me news related to my research.

When I was a member of a group as a researcher I could also participate in their internal discussions. It seems that apart from the formal assemblies, the use of internet platforms allowed the assemblies or the debates to extend in time, providing opportunities for deliberation over a topic that people needed time to reflect upon. The same variable use of internet tools allowed quick coordination in case any issue needed quick resolution.

There are people who do not use the internet at all, or use it at a minimum. Moreover, the use of each technological means might vary through time for each person who is active in this grassroots economy. Some people use social media a great deal for some period of time, but then they are not interested in using the platform anymore, because they got tired or because they are busy and/or their other responsibilities have increased.

What was made clear by my research participants, both through observation and then through interviews and mostly through the questionnaire survey I did during my PhD research, was that most people have access to a mobile phone and in most cases to the internet. Access to the internet might not be regular, and low or unstable income can mean that people do not have regular access to the mobile services either. In many initiatives, special care and procedures are undertaken by the initiatives to support people without access to internet or with limited experience with ICT technologies. Special tutorials, whether live or online, are prepared for members to learn how to use parallel currency software. And there is secretarial support for people who have no internet access but want to register the transactions digitally after each transaction has been registered manually on special paper vouchers.

It is obvious that parallel currency schemes, which represent an activity where there is a specific accounting unit adopted in order to account for the value of the transactions of the members, have higher needs for online platforms and specialized software than a free bazaar. The free bazaar, in particular a bazaar that is not permanent, that is, it does not need a physical venue with people to show the guests around, has no accounting unit, and the digital technologies that are needed in reality are those for organizing the event. Given that the initiative itself does not aspire to count values, there is no need for extensive accounting and accounting technology.

Time banks might have a special platform or software or they might use simple spreadsheets, especially if they do not have many members. Social kitchens or social clinics might be digitized or not, depending on the group's choices. There are solidarity/sharing initiatives that avoid digitization and initiatives that prefer it because it allows better and quicker management of the materials they use in their activities, which is the case with social clinics that have to manage and safeguard medicinal substances.

The general tendency is, however, that what can be done without internet and without digital technologies probably will be done without those technologies. This allows better participation of people without access to digital gadgets and to internet, even if it might slow down processes at some point. It seems that digitization is not a priority nor is it something that is seen as able to resolve issues on its own. I also think that people prefer to avoid digitization, because the precision it entails or enables might be something they are not very fond of, or as I have explained previously, it is not something that they want in their activities. In that way, whenever one sees digital technology being used, that means that this is usually the least use people can make of it in order to achieve their goals within the initiative they are members of.

Nevertheless, it seems that this type of economic activity is very well linked to internet, as the about 8% of questionnaires from my PhD research revealed. The survey questionnaire circulated mostly online, through the various grassroots economic initiatives that exist in Greece in 2011. I did not send the questionnaire to any people who were not members of initiatives and, in most cases, the initiatives' coordinators were those to disseminate the link of the questionnaire to each initiative's members. Yet, it seems that the questionnaire link circulated 'on its own' beyond the initiatives (and I do not think that my posting of it on my research account on Facebook affected that much its dissemination). It is not clear how this occurred, but many people who have internet access learned about the research and wanted to participate, answer the questions and share their views about their activities in the non-mainstream transaction world. I cannot know whether they learned about the research by word of mouth and then found the questionnaire online or whether they learned about the research only through the internet because at that time (autumn 2011) many people were sharing the link of the questionnaire on their own initiative, at their websites and/or personal accounts on social media (Sotiropoulou 2012a: 169–244).

I got a similar impression from research I conducted after my PhD had been completed (2012). People use internet and social media platforms in various ways, and it is always in ways that fit their purposes rather than using ICTs for showing off. Showing off can also happen sometimes – and I understand it. I mean, it is completely normal for people to want to showcase their group, attract attention and new members, and intervene in public debates as a group. However, from my research I know that the work needed in this type of initiatives is of such volume and complexity that there is no time for showing off only. Some (very few) initiatives that chose to invest more time in public relations than in doing the work they needed to do according to their objectives, did not have the practical results they wanted or their public image was promising. In practice, the work of establishing and running such an initiative is extensive and most people prefer to do this by priority. In no case do the websites of an initiative reflect the real work that the group members have done. Even in cases where the groups update their sites regularly, the updates do not at all reflect the work done on the ground.

Generally, it seems that all types of initiatives use internet in one way or another, even if it is done by some members of a group and the rest of the members are notified by other means or technologies. In the case of emergency organizing, such as to support refugees or to support people affected by a disaster, people organize at least part of the grassroots channelling of resources and support needed through internet because this is the quickest and cheapest way to do it. They employ social media, email lists or online announcements on websites that then are re-posted in social media accounts either directly or as image files or just copy-pasted texts. The information shared mentions what needs are imminent, sometimes enumerating in detail what types of clothes, medicines or food are needed. The same announcements mention why they do not need other types of stuff or whether some items are needed in bigger quantities than other items and whether a need has been covered or there are materials in excess. A great deal of information is shared concerning where to offer the items to be shared and where to find collection points in one's area (with online mapping having become a collective digital creation, too). The announcements also give information about where the collected items have been directed, or where the senders can direct what is no longer needed in one place but is still needed in other areas, and how those items can be transported.

The flexibility that this type of announcements allows is of utmost importance in times of emergency because with simple statements news can be disseminated through internet. This can be done by people without needing to be members of any initiative. Search machines or posts by friends on social media are usually good starting points for someone to learn about these activities and participate. That means that, in such cases, the internet allows creation of networks of solidarity without a formal group to be needed to exist. Or, if there are groups involved in this, they are very decentralized in terms of both geography but also activity or type of action undertaken.

For example, in order to support refugees with winter accessories that were dearly needed in winter 2015–2016, there was a social media group that allowed people to self-organize knitting groups all over the country. The same group could use simple announcements to channel offers of yarn by those who had not any time or skills to hand-knit the clothes needed, to those living nearby but had no ability to buy yarn. Then the same group was giving information on how people in various regions could send the handmade goods *en masse* to the points where refugees were trying to survive. The transport was made by free courier services offered especially for the case even by private companies, which made sure that the knitted items reached the geographical points where refugees were passing through (or were trapped in).[1]

The first observation is that people involved in non-mainstream modes of transaction, production and distribution use all types of platforms and communication tools. From mobile phones to social media and from trivial software for poster design to specialized open-source software for parallel currency management and use, everything is tried or used, depending on the needs and aims each group has at a certain point of time. The initiatives' members use what is available and what is appropriate in each case, with a lot of creativity and inventiveness in using tools with as much simplicity as possible.

This shows that they are very good in understanding the machines they can access in their homes, in their workplaces or in the leisure spaces as means of economic activity that can be used to various economic ends. In particular, they are very good at re-imagining and repurposing those same machines used in a capitalist setting, to become active in economic arrangements that aspire to be more egalitarian, sharing-oriented and environment-friendly.

They also look first at the ends they want to reach, in order to select their means in each case. This shows that quantification and measuring is just one aspect of the use of the technological tools they have at hand, but it is not their main aim. In other words, they do not seem to be thinking of machines as quantification tyrants, as most critical theorists perceive them. If the people of the grassroots economic initiatives think of them in that way, they reduce or limit the use of the machine instead of discarding them or instead of using them the way the same tools are used in capitalist production. Moreover, precisely because their approach to quantity and measuring is variable, the technological means they use for this purpose also vary, or they might not be used at all for measuring or accounting purposes that capitalist production would prefer to perform through the use of ICTs.

The second observation is that the members of the grassroots initiatives consider live interaction to be the best way to communicate and also to be economically active. Some participants make this point directly and explicitly during discussions. This makes sense especially when people are involved in activities where neither pricing nor other accounting means exist.

If you want, for example, to collectively cultivate a field, the best way to do it is to meet the people you want to work with, and use emails or mobile phones to organize details after the main arrangements have been done live. Information and communication technologies are seen as complementary, even if the activity itself is practically based on them, as in the case of free online networks or the mapping of collection points for refugee support in 2015. For example, people were also asking around about collection points and transport options, or they were visiting the spaces of local grassroots movements to ask for information and speak with people who already were organizing the support.

This balanced stance towards quantity and towards machinery, but also towards the potential or danger of digital technologies to become arbiters of everything economic and everything measurable, is something that is highly visible in this kind of economic activity. It is also a balanced stance that allows people to use the ICTs the way they feel comfortable with. There are ICT experts in the groups who are very well connected with the technology, and people view them with respect and also assign them to do things that allow their connection to the technology to continue. Therefore, the people who are members of the groups are not forced into a technological abstention and the technological tools are well appreciated in all cases. It means that if ICTs are a means of production (and they are), those are intended to become available to all as much as possible. Then, people are free to choose to use them more or less, depending on their preferences and personal and collective circumstances.

There are very few people who do not want to use digital technologies at all in this type of economic activity. This usually happens either because they find it boring or because they have other reasons. Some other members do most of their grassroots economic activity through digital technologies, but they seem to be a small number compared to people who use digital technologies following their at-the-time needs. This accommodation of all types of use of technologies is very flexible but also very humane. In contrast to the usual capitalist workspaces where employees have to use technologies that they do not like or which they find useless and time-consuming, the grassroots economic initiatives allow people to explore the digital tools. They allow their members to learn the technologies if they can and if they want and decide about the extent to which those tools are useful for their personal and collective activity. As I have written in this chapter, I can attest personally that I was trained to do this by my participants with reference to social media.

9

Machines otherwise?

In the previous chapters we showed how people who use digital technologies and the machines related to them are able to differentiate the use of those machines along with differentiating the measuring practices while they use those machines. This differentiation and adaptiveness of machines or means of production and transaction or distribution is linked to the stance taken by the people who use them. The stance could be named critical, balanced or inventive with reference to technologies and practices.

This stance becomes a possibility or is created collectively because the people who participate in those grassroots initiatives have much more control over the technology they use than in other production spaces. That is, they can decide about the aims of production, the outcome of the production process, the distribution process and even about the use of what has been produced in many cases. They can also decide the extent of their involvement with the production and distribution, according to their needs or life cycles. Even when there are problems concerning the workload in a group or initiative (Sotiropoulou 2016a, 2020b), the people participating in it have, in a practical sense, more negotiating power than in a usual capitalist working space.

Within this context, the whole set of technological tools takes different roles than the roles in production and distribution processes where the producers have much less control concerning their work. No doubt, there are limitations to those roles or uses, as we shall see in the next chapters. There are also challenges and problems because grassroots economic initiatives are not spaces where the capitalist patriarchal hierarchies are not present.

Nevertheless, we need to compare this grassroots use of technologies and measurement to the use that capitalist patriarchy does to the same tools and the same measuring practices or, to be more accurate, to the same measures. There is a huge question mark at this point, whether we are really talking about the same measures.

For example, the time accounted as working time in a capitalist work space – let's say a factory or in a delivery platform (like the ones under the label of 'gig economy') – is counted with the same time hours as the ones used in a time bank. I mean, the time measure is formally the same, but the use of it is very different. Both are capitalist patriarchal times, in the sense that they are counted with precision by the same clocks.

Deep down, the perception of time as a measure does not differ much in the two cases, which raises huge questions about the non-capitalist character of the time banks. After all, counting time hours with precision is a very capitalist practice, embedded in modernity, colonialism and in the perception of time as a resource that needs to be used efficiently for the sake of productivity. The cases of people who participate in time banks and feel reluctant to register the hours they offer, mean that even the time bank members have this perception of how the accounting character of time is problematic. Time bank coordinators sometimes complain about members not wanting to register their transactions. This negative stance towards the accounting of time offered is one more example of how much the people who participate in this type of scheme are aware of the problematic structure of time as a measure.

The same discussion about time can be amplified concerning the type of calendars used in the transactions or in arrangements of reciprocity or contribution to a collective effort. Both capitalist patriarchy and the economic arrangements aspiring to be much better than the former use the solar calendar and the lunar calendar. That capitalism is not especially conscious about the use of lunar calendars does not make the use any less capitalist.

However, the same calendars have a different role in the economic activity, when the people who use them create long-term arrangements for flexible transactions instead of demanding immediate remuneration. The perception of deadline is not prominent, in full contrast to the capitalist perception of due delivery of obligations. In the free bazaars on the other hand, given that remuneration is not required, the calendar is used only to make sure that people learn when the event will take place, with the intention to attract as many people as possible so that they can get what they need and bring what they do not need. In that case, precision is not that necessary, but obviously people need to gather on the same day and hour span to participate in order for the sharing to succeed.

There are cases where precision is necessary, in order to facilitate both the collective production but also to support the most vulnerable of the members of the initiative. An example is the work done in a social clinic or social kitchen: if the health workers are not on time or if the cooked food is not ready at the time that people know it will be shared, there will be serious problems in the provision of the goods that the collective effort is intended to distribute. However, we also saw that the machine uses along with measures are not always the same. This is very important, in the sense that in the grassroots economic activity, along with measures and tools that capitalism uses, there are other tools that are used without those being common in capitalist settings. For example, the measures for food (a bag of apples, a basket of spinach, a bottle of vinegar) are used very flexibly in the grassroots schemes but in capitalism they need to follow legal-official measures. In the grassroots schemes, we often find goods sold or offered with generous measures (Gemmill & Mayhew 1995: 81–109). That is, the goods are counted with an official measure (for example a kilogram), but the quantity represented as a kilo is more than the official kilo quantity.

In capitalist distribution/allocation of goods, generous measures are not allowed: foodstuffs are packed or weighted with precision and the producers, that is, the workers, cannot give any more for free unless they have still some control over the allocation process. For example, a small bakery (whether by policy of the owners or by initiative of the employees) can give a biscuit for free to the customer or share spare

bread with the local social kitchen. This is not a possibility for the
workers working in a big bakery workshop or factory. They cannot put
more in each bread bag, and under usual management circumstances
they cannot donate out of their produce, even if they wanted to.

Another example is the zero price for traditional seeds. The
zero price for genetic material for agriculture is something that is
outrageous for capitalism, as long as capitalist production does not take
all profits out of it. At a stage of capitalism where food-production-
related genetic material is pushed to be patented and then sold at a
price, that is, through the use of the official monetary measures, the
abolition of value measuring is itself a measure of value that establishes
the traditional seeds as absolute values. With the term absolute value I
mean here a thing that is 'impossible to be measured', which in a sense
is a measure in itself. Absolute value is not something that is used to
define the value of the product of the seeds, that is, people can sell (for
official currency) the fruit and vegetables produced by those seeds. But
they are not permitted to sell the seeds. In a sense, absolute value is
mostly related to the things most necessary for a society to survive –
let's call them essential means of production.

The contrast of those practices with the practices of measuring and
technology use in capitalist production and distribution is huge. In
capitalist production, certain machines, technologies and measures are
used or manipulated so that value is created and transferred from the
working classes to the capitalist class. This is why only certain measures
are useful for capitalism and only certain uses of the machines are
acceptable, under the labels of *efficient* and *rational*. This is also why
those certain uses of measures and machines are obligatory for workers.
The producers of wealth in that case cannot opt out of using a certain
technology. They cannot refuse to reply to their boss's emails and they
cannot not login to the application that tracks their working pathway
and pace while they deliver parcels to clients.

The people in the grassroots initiatives can refuse to use technologies
they do not like or which they are not happy to use for any reason. In
cases where high mechanization of the activity is chosen, this happens

after a collective decision. Even if the decision proves to be problematic, it is still a decision that the group made for themselves and can revisit at will. Change of software, experimentation with other tools, discarding practices that seem not to work is much easier in a grassroots group than in a capitalist workspace. It is also common to have group members helping each other with the use of digital technologies and creating options for those who are not especially confident with that use.

An argument could be made that the stakes are not that high and that the aims are different, that is, efficiency is not required and productivity is not necessary. However, in practice the stakes are also huge: they are stakes of personal and collective survival. Although the initiatives are small scale, the possibilities they create for people to cover basic needs (including socializing and collective belonging) mean that if the food is not produced and distributed adequately in a social kitchen many people will go hungry. For the same reasons, efficiency and productivity are also connected to survival. I doubt whether the profit making of the capitalist is a stronger motive than people working to make a living. And this is why capitalism likes to keep the majority of workers in poverty and extorts more surplus value in times of crisis, when workers have to work harder to keep the businesses for which they work afloat.

In the grassroots economic initiatives, however, profit is not a main motive, and is usually not a motive at all. If capitalists make any profit out of this activity, this is done in a completely different way than the direct accumulation of surplus value in a capitalist business, as we shall see in the next chapters.

Therefore, the different measures or uses of measures, and the different ways of using technologies and machines, are connected to the different aims that the economic arrangements are built upon. Whether the aims are achieved is a huge ongoing discussion that is also explored in the next chapters. What is important at this point is to see the use of the machines and measurement potential within the framework that this type of economic activity creates. We need to bear in mind that the avoidance or limited use of quantification tools is not something that does not happen in more mainstream settings (Arjaliès & Bansal

2018, Diamond & Hausman 1994, Hull 2015, Labatut et al. 2011, Moore 2011). However, as with the grassroots use of measurements and technology, the information and understandings we have about those cases are quite limited.

First, when people are involved in non-mainstream modes of production, transaction and/or distribution, they are very creative and inventive in how they are going to use digital technologies to achieve their aims. Everything in reality depends on the situation they are in and on the general conditions they want to tackle. The same people might use different digital tools in order to participate in a parallel currency and different digital tools to participate in a free bazaar. Moreover, the same grassroots initiative might use different tools or platforms to have a picture about their own activity for internal management and coordination purposes and different tools to negotiate their activity with people who are not members.

The variety of tools and measuring practices is taking place on individual and collective levels and creates interconnections not only between people as individuals and between individuals and collectives, but also between the tools themselves and the practices they are employed in. In that way, and well before most mobile phones had connection to internet, the mobile phones were used to notify about material that was shared through internet or to request a transaction after the information of the offer was found online. In many cases this combination of machines and technologies persists even if (or because of) most mobiles now are connected to internet, because, as I have mentioned before, live communication is preferred if it is possible.

Second, given that the stance towards quantification and measurement is very different from what happens in the mainstream economy, the machine use follows the patterns of the activity. The case of parallel currencies is a good example in this case. It seems that the currency structure is imposing itself on the aims of the schemes and the needs of many people who participate in those schemes. The association of the parallel currency with the official currency and the assumption that free markets can function properly if left on their own defines most of the currency schemes. This does not seem to be a fault of the machines or of the software used, but of the entire design of the currency.

It is also a problem of measure. If the parallel currency assumes the same value measures as the official currency, the accounting done through the digital machine cannot give very different results than the ones it would give with the same value measures in the mainstream capitalist patriarchal economy. If you devalue the production of food, for example, the digital technology cannot increase the value of food production on its own. This type of measuring and accounting of value would be problematic with and without digital technologies. It is possible that the use of digital technologies can show the monetary problems much quicker than other accounting technologies, and they literally do so in a very visible, tangible manner (Sotiropoulou 2014b).

This ability of digital technologies to make monetary flows more visible in a quicker manner than before raises important questions about nice stories of parallel currencies in the past, especially during the mid-war period in Europe and US. Maybe the lack of such technology at that time did not show the problems of valuations and other injustices that the digital machines now expose when we create a parallel currency. The appreciation of older cases of parallel currencies needs to be done with attention and care exactly because we now see how easily a currency can turn against the very people it is supposed to help.

The same care and attention are needed now for the contemporary schemes. The assumption that parallel currency schemes were more successful in the past but now for some 'unknown' reason the schemes are not so effective, needs to be examined through the use of technologies that can provide us better information on what is happening with a currency scheme in real time. In the case of parallel currencies made digital, the communities who use them cannot avoid the accumulation of information on the ways their system works. The information is there, and even if the community want to postpone critical discussions or even if they want to experiment more with any initial design they have chosen, they cannot avoid the challenges that are documented because of the technological tools that are used.

Third, the more an activity diverges from what we think of as economic action in mainstream economics, the more the measuring practices elude the technologies used. In other words, the more distant an economic activity is from capitalist patriarchal settings and tends to be a horizontally governed collective production and sharing practice, the more the contemporary technologies are put aside as complementary and they are not used to quantify the activity as such. Or, they are used to quantify only certain parts of the activity, like the digitization of medical supply stocks in some social clinics.

I have just mentioned the example of parallel currency schemes and how their monetary character makes them more prone to reproduce capitalist patriarchal valuations. That the scheme members choose to peg the parallel currency to the official currency makes things worse and more quickly so, because the valuations made in official currency are immediately transposed in the parallel currency. The same type of activities, that is, currencies, are the least able to attract people who might be the most vulnerable or people who have no EU citizenship. The currency schemes require registration and this impedes the participation of people who might have ended up being undocumented immigrants, usually after remaining unemployed for a long time and losing their residence permits. The need to account for the transactions in a more or less precise manner requires that people are identified, and this makes the most vulnerable people afraid to participate, because at any time the authorities might seize the lists of members.

On the other hand, solidarity structures like social kitchens and social clinics where all production and distribution are not done through money-based accounting are very good in attracting and involving people who might not be EU citizens, and feel much safer to participate in such an initiative. Just like free bazaars, those initiatives are also more likely to prepare announcements and leaflets in languages other than Greek.

It seems that collective production and distribution makes sense to involve people who are in a vulnerable position and it is meaningful for them to participate and produce there rather than register with a currency scheme. Solidarity initiatives do not have a registry of members and even the social clinics treat people without asking for residence documents or divulging their details to authorities. The solidarity initiatives do not have accounts for their members in the usual sense of a parallel currency scheme, and they do not account for money because they consistently avoid donations in money.

Even for monetary donations, if any, a social kitchen might announce the donation online, on their Facebook group. In most cases the donors do not want their names to be mentioned, but the donation amount is announced for transparency purposes, even if the donors' names are not mentioned. The group members afterwards discuss the use of the donated stuff or money only in the group's assembly, where all quantities are discussed: how much food is available and for how much time in the future; whether a local business decided to offer more food for free or better raw materials at low or zero price; whether more kitchenware is needed; whether any money donated needs to be used to buy baby food for some families in need; or whether there are enough people to cook and share the food for the next weeks. Even the monetary donation in such cases is immediately turned to kind, that is, materials needed, and is discussed immediately as materials that will soon be bought by the collective.

Therefore, the use of machines and measuring in a solidarity initiative is limited to accounting for those quantities that are necessary for the group and the activity. Depending on the scope and aims of each initiative, there are quantities and measures that are ever-present with small variations in most initiatives, but in reality they are not digitized. In many cases, the group members prefer to let each other know about what materials are missing, whether the work shifts need rescheduling and what materials have been acquired or donated. This sharing of information among members is where most of the digital technology is involved.

In most cases the quantities that are necessary for the group to perform their tasks are not written down at all, or they are written down very informally. The reason is that the common management and the assembly usually seem to be adequate as management committee and accountability mechanism. Even in cases where issues of mismanagement and misuse of resources arise, digitization is never discussed as a solution. It seems impractical, but also offending for all members. This is understandable particularly if one takes into account that precision and obligatory remuneration are already understood as such (impractical and offending).

In other words, the people do not use the machines to measure their activity as a priority of the use. Their main aim is to make sure that communication and coordination of the people involved is effective despite or because of the fact that the activity uses other types of measuring or avoids measuring entirely.

The question whether the digital technologies have made this activity possible in the first place, or only visible to society (and academics in particular) while the activity existed before them, requires a separate study in its own right, as has already been mentioned. There is a possibility that this type of economic activity took a new boost because of the new information and communication technologies, but this needs to be investigated as well.

What one could say at this point is that visibility is a huge contribution to the activity. Visibility reversed or at least debilitated the stereotypes of ignorance, poverty, inefficiency and unidimensional backwardness that have been associated with non-monetary or multi-monetary economic activity during modernity and capitalist expansion (Sotiropoulou 2012b). It also created challenges to various sections of critical theory, because the grassroots activities, by becoming visible, cannot be ignored and cannot easily fit in most existing theories about the economy or theories about resistances to capitalism. Even if the theorists do not want to discuss what is really happening in terms of economic experiments and economic arrangements in grassroots initiatives, the people who participate and also their communities can learn how the initiatives function much more easily. If theory does not care to understand, if theorists do not find the details of the activities important enough to rethink the economy, the people themselves will do it anyway because they have to. Either because they participate or because they witness the activity, they are involved in the thinking about it and they are also the pioneers who do that thinking.

Part Three

Machines, measures and (social) reproduction

We have seen in the previous chapters various examples in detail, of how the use of machines and measures takes place in grassroots economic initiatives. The amazing work that has been and is still being done is undoubtedly a collective achievement that creates many possibilities concerning collective organizing and collective economic arrangements.

However, we need to not lose the perception of the whole and how those same initiatives have to exist within a context that is favourable neither to them nor to their aims. The next chapters are not written in order to bring pessimism to the debate. Much less are they added to the book to balance out the positive understandings of the previous Part 2.

The next chapters are an attempt to understand the challenges the grassroots initiatives face and how the technologies they use are not neutral but embedded within a social and economic system just as everything and everyone else are. The possibilities and achievements in terms of practice and theory are precarious if we do not examine what is at stake in this case. With the same care that we recognize the creativity and inventiveness of the people who participate in grassroots groups and use measures and digital technologies to achieve their aims, with that same care we need to recognize systemic injustices and existing structures that function against those aims and see (that is, discuss, collectively) how to supersede them.

10

Machines, measures and the neoliberal version of capitalist patriarchy

One question that has emerged consistently since 2009 is whether all those grassroots initiatives have been a direct result of crisis. In many cases this causal link is taken as given. In other cases, it is assumed to be quite normal, that is, that people always do this when there is a problem with the economy. In most cases, the assumption that poverty induced by capitalist restructuring is enough a reason for people to undertake this economic activity proliferates in various types of texts, within and outside academia.

The problem with this assumption and the direct causality it is based on is that it is inaccurate in so many ways that sometimes it feels hopeless to attempt to debunk the points of which the assumption consists. It assumes that what we have seen in detail in the previous chapters, both as practice and as creation of ideas about the economy 'in the field', has been created by contemporary neoliberalism one way or another. But what happened with neoliberalism in Greece during these last 15 years?

In the first place, the capitalist patriarchal social reproduction crisis was already in advance in Europe and elsewhere. As we have seen in the first part of the book, that crisis was structural anyway. Given that Greece is generally a capitalist economy and well connected with other major capitalist economies in Europe, the structural crisis would not be avoided. Quite the opposite: the participation of Greece in the Eurozone was expected to bring many problems to the country, exactly because its economic development was not similar to the wealthiest countries of the zone. That had been known since Greece joined the Eurozone. The theory of optimum currency areas upon which the Eurozone has been constructed included a warning about the problems that poor countries or regions in a common currency area would face: they would become the buffer zones of the currency area in any crisis that would emerge in its economy (Mundell 1961).

Just like there are various forms of capitalism, the neoliberal restructuring that was labelled as crisis after 2008 took specific forms in Greece. Some of them were shared in common with neoliberal restructurings in other countries, and some of them were local, in the sense that they were linked to how capitalism functions in the Greek economy. The neoliberal policies adopted in Greece since 2008 revealed the locally existing capitalist patriarchal contradictions with all their successes and failures. But they also revealed local resistances that possibly existed well before 2008 but were not perceived as such or were not perceived as existing at all.

The signing of a series of Memoranda and associated debt bailout agreements by Greece and the 'troika' of IMF, EU and ECB since 2010 onwards, led to the acceleration of neoliberal restructuring of the economy. The restructuring was not a newly introduced process. It had started officially with Greece becoming a member state of the European Economic Community in 1981 and intensified after 1992, when the Maastricht Treaty was signed. Greece started using the euro currency in 2002, which heavily enhanced the neoliberal orientation of the economy. The stability pact criteria were directly connected to austerity, public expenditure cuts, and privatizations well before 2008 (Featherstone 2005, Hadjimichalis & Vaiou 1990, Karaliotas 2017).

When the 2008 crisis erupted and in particular after 2010 when the first memorandum was signed, we saw the imposition of even harsher economic conditions onto the most vulnerable groups of the population. Loss of GDP was massive and increase of poverty and unemployment were some of the most visible results of those polices. Given that private banks were bailed out with public funds and then the Greek state had to borrow more funds from abroad, public funds were not directed to the already limited and problematic social welfare state services and basic infrastructure like schools and hospitals. The cuts in public expenditures included the decrease or elimination of support to people with disabilities, severe health conditions, or to families with many dependents and the elderly.

The above induced an abrupt increase in needs of basic survival because people lost income in the economy and at the same time they could not use public services that were also curtailed. In reality, there has been a privatization of care work, that was dumped upon the household members, given that the households had to cope with care needs that the public services would not cover anymore. Women have been the social group that was mostly burdened with this extra work. The reason is not only the patriarchal structure of many Greek communities but also the clearly patriarchal character of the Greek state. Particularly, the welfare state is an example of familial type, where the whole design of welfare assumes that families, that is, women, are doing the vast part, if not most, of the care labour in the country.

Women and anyone else who was doing care work before 2010, when the first memorandum (bailout agreement) was signed, found themselves trapped in a situation that was already bad. It got worse because women and all care workers, whether paid or unpaid, had to cope with the reduction of public services and welfare transfers. Moreover, the public expenditure cuts meant that many care workers, who are also by majority women, were left unemployed or underemployed in precarious employment and unemployment conditions. Precarious employment with all its repercussions (deterioration of working conditions, poverty and non-registered unemployment) increased due to the further deregulation of job markets (Anagnostopoulos & Siebert 2015, Pagones 2013).

The needs for care work did not decrease of course. Hence, much of the work that was previously undertaken in terms of resources and remuneration for the work done as a social obligation through the state policies, became unpaid and a responsibility of families and communities instead of the state.

Within this context the people who were living in Greece as migrant workers were brought into an even worse situation. The immigrant workers have been the first to be fired or/and to have their meagre incomes further minimized. They were also the first to be forced to enter a very dangerous precariousness with the unemployment and poverty on the one hand, and the EU and Greek state (anti) immigration policies, plus the neo-Nazi violence, against them, on the other. Unemployed immigrants lose their rights to residence but also to healthcare, which makes them vulnerable to state violence and to Nazi violence, because they cannot report Nazi attacks to the authorities, for the fear of being arrested and deported or held in detention centres for undocumented migrants.

This fear also makes them very vulnerable to local (that is, Greek) employers, because immigrant workers have to find any job under any conditions (well below any legally regulated level of wage or working conditions) to be able to have their residence documents renewed. Many immigrant workers are doing care work, and in general they work in reproduction sectors, like food production, construction and of course domestic and care labour of all kinds. This means that they are also not well paid and that the reduction of the economic activity that austerity induced found them in already precarious conditions with not enough savings or negotiating power.

Under such conditions faced by all worker classes in Greece, the measurement practices of capitalist patriarchy took a very particular character that intensified the transfer of wealth from the many to the few and from the producers, that is, workers, to the capitalists, that is, owners of means of production and means of discipline (capital and institutions that impose violence on workers). The debt obligations of the capitalist state therefore became obligations of the workers classes that would be tamed to bear the costs of it (Glenn 2019: 43–76 & 153–92, Graeber 2011, Lazzarato 2011). Measuring and quantities became a very common tool in the mainstream political discourse, especially when the person who was speaking was in favour of austerity policies.

Neoliberal restructuring meant that every public service was considered merely a cost for the public budget. Healthcare and education, welfare services and public infrastructure along with infrastructure repair and management have all been labelled as costs for the economy and the state budget, with devastating effects on the population (Karanikolos et al. 2014). The discourse did not change in 2020 when the Covid-19 pandemic broke out. That means, the choice of counting the wages of the doctors and nurses as costs was a long-term policy choice that would not change even if the results of the expenditure cuts in healthcare would lead to many thousands of deaths that could have been avoided (Lytras & Tsiodras 2022, Lytras 2022).

The attack to the worker classes also took the form of attacking nature and privatizing sites or public goods that before were commons, either dedicated to common use, or public property, that is, state property managed by public services. Privatizations of nature and public or common goods were not new in Greece either, but after 2010 the policy became even more aggressive and expansive, at the expense of those who have the least economic and financial means to get by (Apostolopoulou & Adams 2015, Pempetzoglou & Patergiannaki 2017, van den Berge et al. 2019)

The public expenditure cuts did not mean that the state reduced state functions that were necessary for the neoliberal policies to be implemented. Austerity included the redirection of public funds to policing and suppression of dissent (Giniger & Sotiropoulou 2019). Generous purchases of means for producing state violence, that is, public physical discipline, increased and never stopped, even while the Covid-19 pandemic showed that there were dire need to invest in healthcare (which did not happen). New police personnel were hired at increasing numbers. The purchases of multitude (protest) suppression equipment by the Greek police and the maintaining of salaries (or creating new positions) for policemen shadow the lack of basic medicinal materials in hospitals and heating in schools. At the same time, as we have already mentioned, the medical, social care and teaching personnel in the public sector have been reduced and also saw their working conditions, including their salaries, reduced and worsened.

One of the most important measures that were used to justify the austerity policies has been public debt. Public debt is the amount of money that the government owes. Greek public debt expanded due to bailing out the (private) Greek banks, which continued to be private with private management (therefore, the state did not take over the control of them). Bailing out the private banks meant that the state needed to borrow more, because there were no longer enough funds nor enough income to pay other previous debts. The reduction in economic activity and the increased unemployment also meant that the state lost a significant amount of tax income, even if it increased the taxes (both in scope and volume). The disruption to the economy was such that even seen from the capitalist point of view the austerity policies did more harm to the overall economy than good (Kapitsinis 2022, Koratzanis & Pierros 2017).

The over-indebted government/Greek state meant that this quantity (of debt) and the inability of the state to sustain repayment on both the previous and the new debts (for bailing out the Greek banks) led to a massive quantification (and at ridiculous prices) of everything that belongs to the Greek state: real estate property, non private-propertied common goods like islands, forests, rivers, or even archaeological sites. All public property became a set of measurable and monetarily-valued assets on sale under the administration of Hellenic Republic Asset Development Fund (HRADF – ΤΑΙΠΕΔ). HRADF is the public agency responsible to create income on behalf of the 'creditors' of the Greek state by selling public properties to private investors, or by letting public goods and infrastructure for such a long term that it is more or less equal to selling. Some of the public properties cannot be sold, in the sense that they cannot be a private property through conveyancing property rights, but they can be privatized by selling the usufruct rights (leasing) of the good for many decades with exclusive powers transferred to the buyer. Therefore, in practice it is a privatization and sellout (Glenn 2019: 153–92, Karaliotas 2017, Velegrakis et al. 2015).

Putting a price on previously public and priceless items was a mental exercise not only for the neoliberalism-oriented policy-makers, technocrats and mass media presenters, but also for the entire Greek society, which had to accept the pricing as normal. Whether the pricing was accepted and legitimized or not, the pricing was legal, in the sense that it was adopted by law.

The monetization of various public goods and infrastructure created a peculiar situation. On the one hand, the debate whether this is right and how we could avoid the pricing and privatization whatsoever was ongoing. On the other hand, in the same debates, the very low prices were also discussed. It seemed that the monetization of public assets was also a direct devaluation of them.

At the same time, the entire scope of human life and well-being were accounted as costs on their own right. Access to necessary medical tests and medicines for people with serious illnesses such as cancer and HIV-AIDS were limited to extent of elimination (of both the services and the patients). That this was done not without protests and resistance by both patients and health workers does not mean that the policy was repelled as we would have hoped. Even today, hospitals in Greece occasionally refer their patient to social clinics (the ones organized on the basis of non-monetary activity that we described in the previous chapters) to receive medicines or care that is not available in public hospitals. This has been even more necessary for people who lost their healthcare cover by the public healthcare system because of unemployment. For immigrant workers, who were also in danger of being reported to the police or who did not have any healthcare access, sometimes, not even in a case of emergency, the social clinics (that is, the grassroots organized health centres) were their only remedy for all their healthcare issues (Cabot 2016).

There have been many infuriating cases of policies adopted within this logic which conflated healthcare provision with costs. It was necessary for the public to make a huge fuss when the Greek state decided that it is too costly to cover the expenses for special shoes for patients with diabetes. The policy-makers found out that in many cases, the patients who use special shoes for some years might have to resort to an amputation in the future, if their diabetes intensifies. Therefore, they adopted legislation that cut the expenditures for those special shoes and suggested the amputation of feet/legs even if it was not necessary because the legs of the patients were still healthy, and were expected to be healthy for several years to come if they could use the special shoes. That was the solution chosen in order to avoid the costs of providing the shoes that would make the amputation operation either redundant or postponed for a certain period of time. That the resistance of the citizens made the government change this decision does not make the initial decision any better (Ntouka 2010).

The same mentality was explicitly demonstrated during the Covid-19 pandemic. The government reduced the budget for healthcare instead of increasing it. They left health personnel without proper equipment, without payment and/or without contracts (that is, they continued the layoff of health personnel as it was scheduled before the pandemic). The healthcare expenditure costs that were not undertaken were directed to hiring even more police personnel and police equipment, as if nothing extraordinary related to public health was happening (Georgakopoulos 2021). That the neoliberal policies had created a situation where the Covid-19 pandemic would hit the worker classes hard and the economy of the country would not be able to recover soon, not even according to capitalist metrics, was more than expected (Maris & Flouros 2022).

In this chapter we raised the question about those policies and their connection, possibly causal, with the different measuring and machine or technology use in the grassroots economic initiatives. The question holds for all activity that has a grassroots economic character. Because this is a very important question and very much related to the role that those measuring practices, valuations, and uses of technologies have in the greater capitalist context, we will discuss it in the next chapter. At this stage, there is one point to make: the quantification was fundamental for the neoliberal restructuring, in Greece, and elsewhere.

Machines and measures in service of (social) reproduction

Under those conditions, having social clinics where healthcare is provided without even asking for the ID card of the patient (that would place undocumented migrants in danger of being arrested) is a materially expressed reversal of capitalist patriarchal valuations. Strict measuring is used in order to calculate the amount of medicinal substances for treating a condition but not in calculating the cost of the service provided. The cost of the service is conscious and visible, even if the service itself is provided through unpaid labour and through donations. But the cost is not considered to be the responsibility of the patient, that is, the most vulnerable person in the whole situation of healthcare provision.

First, everybody involved in this activity knows that without a social clinic available many people would have no access to healthcare, and their health, well-being and even their lives would be in danger. Second, it is also known that the people who are involved in this type of activity are not wealthy donors and volunteers that have nothing else to fill up their supposedly luxurious free schedule with. Many are also in economic distress but they want to do something with any resources they might have at hand, no matter how meagre those resources might be. They also want to do something about their community, their society. That means, they are not doing this without depriving themselves of resources that are channelled to the grassroots initiatives.

Moreover, their effort, time and stamina are precious for a grassroots initiative, because without them the initiative cannot exist and cannot achieve its aims. Those effort, time and stamina are offered after difficult decisions and after the person who offers them might really have to reproduce themselves in conditions of poverty, unemployment, deprivation and marginalization while contributing to the initiative. I mean, the value of this contribution is beyond price in at least two ways: first, they contribute necessary resources and effort to the community; and, second, they contribute things while they are themselves deprived.

When, therefore, we discuss how solidarity workers are overworked, whether there is a lot of work to do to keep the initiative going, or whether the precision of the time schedule affects the effectiveness of the initiative, we are talking about work done under these kinds of challenging conditions for the group members. Any accounting of those contributions should be made in a way that reflects the setting of the contributions, that is, the hardship within which the individuals and their communities face while people try to organize economic activity in ways whereby everyone survives as well as possible.

Apart from the question as to what is more important to measure – the healthcare as cost or the healthcare as effective practice – the whole activity raises another fundamental question: where quantification is important to use and where it is not. Expressed in another way: the question is in which cases quantity is really protecting the high value of something and in which cases quantification is reducing and delimiting the value of the thing a community values.

I have already mentioned the example of social clinics and of the network that organizes sharing and exchange of traditional seeds. Both the healthcare services in this case and the sharing of traditional seeds with which people can proceed with traditional agriculture and produce food have been assigned a price of zero. It is interesting to see that this zero price is assigned even in spaces where other non-mainstream modes of transaction exist.

That is, people are aware of other modes of assigning value and transacting (like the use of money) and they still want to avoid using those modes for the traditional seeds, for example. Even for the exchange of seeds, this is not really based on obligatory remuneration. Farmers might exchange among themselves (and they can also gift each other with seeds) but those who visit the meeting and have no seeds to offer, take some seeds for free. That is, because traditional seeds have a value that cannot be priced, this non-pricing happens not only in the mainstream, official monetary economy, but also in the non-monetary exchange economy. Because the preservation of seeds presupposes some work and effort, farmers are allowed by priority to have access to them, and this is where limited exchange takes place (but not always – any farmer can give away seeds they have). Apart from that, seeds are free and if one wants to start cultivating them, they are acquired for free. The same happens for those who cannot attend the meeting: they can ask a farmer for seeds they need and they acquire them by paying only the posting fee, provided that the farmer has spare seeds to offer.

This is happening because food and its production along with health are thought to have values that are beyond measure. In reality, the zero price is a signal that measures are not enough in some cases, for example, in ensuring a stable harvest and sound ecosystem or in supporting people's health (Sotiropoulou 2017). This perception of immeasurable value is very important. It is in contrast to the tendency of the last decades to put a price on nature or even on humans and account for them by comparison with the value of other things that they have already been priced. Even ecological economics attempt to price the natural environment and what human societies take or gain from it in order to show that nature is valuable and we need to account for the damage we do to it. This attempt stems from the perception that capitalist patriarchy degrades nature because natural resources are an externality to the economic activity.

By *externality* we mean that natural resources that are used in the economic process are not accounted as costs of the process. Because natural resources are free or quasi-free (that is, we need labour to extract them but nature does not ask for recompense), the real cost of their use is not accounted for in the economy. If the natural resources are internalized in the production process, that is, if they are accounted for, ecological economics says, then we would be able to reveal the real cost of each economic process. Given that some economic activities would be too costly because the damage to nature would be extensive, then the companies would not undertake them. That is, the markets would not accept the excessively high prices of production of certain goods, if those goods had integrated the real prices of the natural resources used in their production.

However, this approach does not account for cases where the damage to nature is irreversible. How much does an ecosystem cost if it is destroyed and we cannot restore it? How much does a resource cost if it is depletable and effectively depleted? It does not even account for the fact that different people and different social groups have different perceptions of comparing values. For example, the tycoon whose company extracts minerals from a region very far away from their own country, might be ready to pay a high price for the minerals knowing that the profits they will make now in their country (that does not suffer the environmental damage) will be enough for their lifetime and for the lifetime of their immediate descendants. In other words, there are some damages that are irreversible for some people but they are not experienced as damages by others.

It is the same with the weighing of healthcare and protection of public health during the times of Covid-19 pandemic. Certain social groups, especially those wealthy enough to access the best healthcare but also to stay away from populous spaces and isolate, had no problem to force worker classes to work for them – and they had no broader perception of what was needed for the pandemic not to lead to the casualties it had. People who could afford to travel, even for entertainment, continued touring abroad for leisure or even for non-essential business. The governments, in Europe at least, in order to 'save the economy' – that is, the capitalist profits and the tight neoliberal welfare government budgets –followed policies that showed explicitly that GDP is more important than healthcare and public health. Factories continued business, although as time went by it was made clear that concentration of people in closed spaces was a virus-spreading facilitator.

For the people who were working in critical sectors, that meant that they would have many casualties and colleagues who recovered at a slow pace after long covid. For the wealthy people this is not a problem because they did not have to work under such conditions, nor were their living conditions degraded before the pandemic, concerning their nutrition, housing quality, quality of open spaces in their neighbourhoods or quality of healthcare. The social groups who were deprived and/or discriminated against before the pandemic bear the burden of the choices of those who could afford to live with less restrictions but would not face the results of their decisions (made in wealth).

Therefore, putting prices on everything means that those who can afford to choose which is the most important thing to pay for, will probably not be those mostly affected by that decision. It also means that putting prices on everything results in pushing domains of life that were not priced or monetized, nor possible to compare with anyone's wealth, to become an abstract quantity into an economy that is highly stratified and supports the accumulation of wealth by the few at the expense of the many and nature.

The cases of grassroots economic activity where people refuse to quantify values and put prices on things they perceive as important are clear examples of how people try to keep outside capitalist accumulation things they consider too important to be allowed to be grabbed by the capitalists (Weiner 1992). They also seem to be aware that there are also other forms of accumulation, that can be non-capitalist but also detrimental to nature and human societies. Their effort to make sure that traditional seeds are freely available even among people who employ non-monetary modes of transaction means that they know that accumulation of agricultural genetic material can take many forms.

In some cases they told me that some decades ago, old farmers did not want to share seeds, but now they have changed their mind. This might have happened because exclusivity in small production in combination with the attack on small production by capitalism brought biodiversity to a breaking point. In one meeting, people were celebrating a very old woman who came herself to bring the seeds she had been holding for years – the moments were thrilling. People told me that her family could not stop her from attending herself even if her mobility was compromised. I still remember her smiling proudly and people clapping around her.

Therefore, the question concerning all the activities I have mentioned in this chapter and in the previous ones, is whether this reproductive activity can only be effective if capitalist patriarchal measures and quantifications are skipped. My position is, based on what I have learned from my research participants, and from social movements in general, that definitely, we cannot use capitalist patriarchal understandings of quantity, much less of value, and be able to effectively reproduce ourselves, the people around us and nature. It is one thing to be aware that we have been educated socially and formally to think and act in capitalist patriarchal measure. It is another thing to know that this education is not the only education and way of thinking we have to employ when we are economically active. This is even more necessary when we want to make sure that our environment and communities will be there the next day, equally well and thriving as yesterday.

It is a third thing to be prepared to get rid of this education as soon as possible if we want to save our local and global livelihoods and to reflect upon the quantity perceptions and measures we invent during that transition period. Maybe there are even more solutions than we can think of now. We will not be able to think of them if we do not experiment, even if our experiments are temporarily linked to capitalist patriarchal measures, valuations and technologies.

The important thing in this discussion is how the use of the same technology that capitalist patriarchy uses is taking another role in this reproductive activity where measures and valuations are different from the mainstream. We have seen those technologies to be used in capitalism in order to account for the value of beaches or for the value of archaeological sites, for the costs of keeping an ill person alive, and for the costs of creating an educated youth. We have every right to be reluctant to use those technologies. At the same time, we might have to reflect on how to resolve problems that the technologies can help us with at the moment, without impeding us to improve our economic arrangements now and in the future.

Therefore, it is important to understand that the no-role of the same machines in measuring quantities that in capitalist patriarchy's value extraction are very relevant, and the refusal to use any measure of value in cases of a good that people deem to be of immeasurable value, IS a measuring practice itself. Actually, quantification starts at the moment one decides what is important to measure, and to what extent. The non-quantified creatures or things are indeed defining what the quantified creatures or things are standing for in terms of measure and what form and volume their quantified character will take.

For example, the value of the traditional seeds' genetic material is not quantified. The seeds, however, that is, the genetic material as such, are quantified slightly ('we have many – this amount of kilos of each species – traditional seeds, but we are going to share them to many people, then we give few seeds to each'). The envelopes for packaging the seeds can be quantified with some precision (in one day, the shared envelopes, each one with separate seed type, may reach an amount of 5,000 or 10,000). Measuring may be done 'by the eye' or by just knowing approximately how many envelopes are used. Apart from that, there is neither will nor wish by the people involved in preserving traditional seeds and traditional cultivation methods to count anything, exactly because the aim is to make the seeds available to many people.

From the above one understands that what prevails is not the machine, but the perception of quantity as a tool itself in a specific economic activity. Nevertheless, just as capitalist patriarchal valuings are articulated with digital technologies to enhance labour monitoring and value accumulation in favour of capital owners, articulations of other types are also taking place in the non-mainstream economic activity. Capitalist patriarchal valuings existed before contemporary information and communication technologies became available. Once the technological tools became easy to use for enhancing capitalist valuation processes and capitalist values, the technology was directed towards those aims by the owners of the means of production, that is, capitalists.

However, the issue of articulation is more complicated than that. Grassroots measuring practices and digital tools are being articulated all the time to cover everyday needs, to face hardships or to experiment with new arrangements, in ways that were not possible some decades ago, even if the measuring practices existed as such. Therefore, a technology that did not exist some decades ago may facilitate a practice that existed but was invisible (at least to mass media and researchers), or it may engender new or modified practices. For example, some decades ago it would have been impossible to have a free online network with people giving away what they do not need and taking what they need, without internet and online interaction platforms. It would only have been possible to share stuff locally even if this would not attract attention by mass media and academics. As mentioned before, this is a possible explanation for the lack of documentation about those practices.

The distinguishing feature between capitalist economic arrangements that prioritize capitalist profit and the economic activity that is the subject-matter of this book is that the tasks and processes this activity entails are central for the reproduction not only of the people involved in it but also of the society and the economy as whole. What the non-mainstream grassroots economic initiatives aspire to is to make sure that people have access, in one way or another, to goods and services that are fundamental for the physical and social survival of the people who participate directly but also of their communities.

It is not a coincidence that the membership in the initiatives, whenever this is formalized with registration procedures, represents individuals in appearance only. Behind and beside every registered member, there is a household and often more than one interconnected households of family members, relatives, friends and neighbours. In terms of class position and gender, most of the people are low or very low income, women are more numerous than men, and the educational level is high. In terms of ethnic background, some initiatives have an extended participation and contribution by people who do not originate from Greece. Other initiatives seem not to have attracted many people who originate from other countries, although all (without exception) initiatives state explicitly that they welcome all people irrespective of origin, language, religion or other background (Sotiropoulou 2012a: 81–126 & 169–244, 2014a, 2016a).[1]

In particular, we see in this type of economic activity that people prioritize food production, healthcare, education. Cultural activities also exist and are very much cherished. It seems, though, that those cultural activities have certain characteristics: protection of nature, grassroots or self-made art, and childcare combined with educational activities. Elderly people are very much welcome and respected in the activities. However, the priority and the major part of the collective effort are directed to cover what we usually call 'necessities', or basic reproduction work that will make sure that the people involved will survive as both biological and social beings in a protected ecosystem. There is conscious organizing so that people's efforts and skills are appreciated, used and developed, within a framework where they do not need official currency to participate in the activity or they use it to a minimum extent (Nembhard 2014, Nembhard & Ifateyo 2014, Sotiropoulou 2011a, 2016a, 2016b, 2015b, 2017).

We have left a question unanswered from the previous chapter: are the crisis of 2008 and the neoliberal policies adopted in Greece since then the creators of all those practices that we discuss here? Is there any causal relationship between those capitalist evolutions and the creation of this type of economic activity?

I have written elsewhere in detail about those questions, but I think that there are some points to make here. The question is valid, in the sense, as I have explained in the previous chapter, that there is an assumption that this type of economic activity is the direct result of the neoliberal policies and of the crisis. This assumption has become a popular narrative in mass media but (or because) it reduces structures and local community knowledge and inventiveness into a reactionary reflex. However, my participants state, and my research findings show, that this activity has deep historical roots in the region, even if economists did not pay attention to it for many decades (Sotiropoulou 2011b, 2012b).

First, one should think what a crisis is and what capitalism is. If we are talking about the Greek state and its economy, there is no time in history since 1830 that the economy was not in one or another form of crisis. The newly established Greek state was already in international debt when it was founded. If the crisis is the cause of this type of activity, then we must look at a crisis that has lasted since 1830 onwards. That does not explain why this type of activity became so extensive or so visible from 2009 onwards.

Second, capitalist restructurings are not new in Greece either. However, if we understand contemporary neoliberalism as a major turn in the evolution of the capitalist system, we also need to see neoliberalism in Greece since it started to be directly implemented as such. Obviously, it did not start in 2009; it is much older than that. Either neoliberalism since 2009 has a specific quality that did not exist before, enough to create all those grassroots initiatives; or we are talking about a system of economic organizing that contributed to the emergence of those groups since 2009 onwards but was not the main reason for that emergence.

Third, to make such historical statements about how anything contributed to the emergence of such an extensive economic activity that defies economic theories, we would need to investigate the economic history of the activity. Up until now such historical research has not been done. I am collecting information but it is impossible to find systematic documentation about this type of economic activity, let alone research writings that cover in a comprehensive way the last 100 years, or maybe the years since 1830 that the Greek state was founded. A lot of the information consists of anecdotal narratives by my research participants but also by people who let me know about older events even if they did not participate in my research in a formal way.

The question will always be: why now; why in those specific regions or geographical points; and most important, why this type of organizing and not another? Along with those questions, there will arise questions about how people knew how to organize; how they could be flexible to use various forms of grassroots economic activity instead of just one (currencies) that the academic literature is so fond of; how they could use digital technologies in such inventive ways; how they could create various ways of measuring, valuing, understanding quantity and implementing quantitative practices, while academics and theorists in general are still struggling to understand what those practices and public statements mean or do in the economy.

As I have already mentioned, I do not think that the activity described in this book is a peculiarity of Greece, but that academic literature and theorists worldwide preferred to pay attention mostly to currencies and see any other measurement tools as currency-like because this is the way capitalist patriarchy understands quantity, that is, through or linked to state-sanctioned money. On the other hand, I understand capitalist patriarchy as a variating political economic system that adapts itself wherever it is imposed, in order to take advantage of local economic structures. The local patriarchal structures are of great value to this system because they are essential to make sure that the capitalist accumulation can take place while having local collaborators who will embrace their new exploitation tools against the people around them. In that sense, capitalist patriarchy is not the same in Greece as in any other country, and no capitalist patriarchy is same as any other. I use the generic term 'capitalist patriarchy' to discuss basic contradictions and social struggles that refer to quantity and machine, while having in mind that similar activities in other countries might take another form.

We must also bear in mind the problematic character of the notion of volunteering with reference to all that work taking place in grassroots initiatives. I have already explained that the people involved in grassroots initiatives are not what the middle-class, Western European, white, privileged notion of volunteering entails. The point in this case is that there is extensive obligation in this type of work. Therefore, the people are forced by the conditions of their life and their community to undertake all this work in order to survive or help other people in their communities survive. Although people join the initiatives on their own and have a lot of flexibility to organize their work, the quasi-obligatory character of the work undertaken means that they proceed in using all those technologies and measuring practices, along with inventing quantity perceptions, because they need to do it.

Therefore, the question is transposed into where this obligation comes from. Is it neoliberalism, which wants or makes people to assign zero price to healthcare and provide it for free to the most disadvantaged? Is it the crisis, which makes them say that traditional seeds are free?

If capitalist patriarchy could, it would allow capitalists to patent all traditional seeds. Proposals for full privatization of everything are not new, and have been circulating widely in academic writings (see for example Demsetz 1964). In a sense, pricing everything, including the oceans or the atmosphere, is part of that privatization process. In that process, if everything has a price, everything can be sold, bought and exclusively used by the buyer.

Therefore, I would definitely disagree that the choices people make in the grassroots economic initiatives are coming from the capitalist patriarchal ravaging that has been happening since 2008. Their choices are clearly directed to finding solutions for social reproduction of humans, their communities, but also for nature. Whether the choices are effective and the grassroots schemes are successful, and if so under which conditions, is a whole debate that we discuss in the next two chapters. It is also a debate that is collective, which means that no matter what position I take, both the success of the initiatives but also the success of creating new perceptions of quantities and measures is a collective effort that has not been finalized yet. This means that my views may hopefully contribute but are not expected to be the most accurate at this stage.

We have shown in different parts of this book that the quantity perceptions, the measures and the technologies people use in the grassroots economic schemes, are aiming at completely different targets and arrangements than those of capitalist patriarchy. We have also shown that the fact that this activity became visible now for various reasons, including the digital technologies we have, does not make the activity a creation of the crisis.

It is true that what people call crisis coincided in time with this type of economic organizing. (Although we must remember that in reality the term *crisis* is used only when economic hardship reaches the middle class, while as long as poverty devastates the workers only, this is not thought of as a crisis.) Its measurings and quantifications, that is, the turn of the public discourse into understanding political decisions through quantities that capitalist patriarchy prefers, coincided with measurings and quantifications that are different and in many cases tend towards other directions than the patriarchal capitalist ones, as we have seen already. Correlation is not causation, however. This coincidence reveals more about the social struggle as expressed through quantifications and valuings rather than about capitalist patriarchy inventing non-capitalist non-patriarchal valuations through reactive citizens who are 'dragged' by the crisis to do all this amazing work.

Therefore, we have a conscious social effort to support social reproduction, which is something that all human societies do and did in their history, in one or another way. That it is done under very harsh conditions and under the aggressive accumulation on the part of capitalists through austerity does not make it any less social. I mean, the social decision to stay alive both biologically but also as societies would exist anyway, with or without capitalism and patriarchy, with or without neoliberalism and with and without the crisis of 2008.

That this decision takes place and is implemented within a framework of capitalist patriarchy, with all the problems and the technologies we have around, does not make capitalist patriarchy the creator of the decision of societies to survive. Much less does it make capitalist patriarchy the creator of modes of production and distribution, but also modes of valuation and quantification that do not support capitalist accumulation.

Even if we accept that patriarchy is the most totalitarian economic system we have experienced until now, we cannot imagine that it is totalitarian enough to think of everything, even of practices that go against it. That capitalist patriarchy always tries to dissolve economic arrangements that do not support its reproduction as a system, or even worse, to co-opt them so that they function at their own expense and at the same time to be turned into arrangements that allow value and wealth to be accumulated by patriarchs and capitalists, is another level of debate that we will discuss in the next chapters.

One thing, therefore, is that social reproduction is under attack by capitalist patriarchy all the time, so that it serves capitalist patriarchy first and then society. Another thing is that capitalist patriarchy is presented as if it supports social reproduction as such for social reproduction purposes and not for its own, capitalist patriarchal ones. That second representation cannot hold. The best that capitalist patriarchy can do is to divert all the work and intellectual effort that all those communities do, to its own benefit. In the next chapters we will discuss some ways in which this diversion takes place or is attempted to take place. As a final comment I would like to add here that we need to be careful when we assign more subjectivity and agency to capitalists because they have more money at hand than the people in communities who try to survive capitalism. We should also be careful to avoid fetishizing machines and technologies (whether machines or social know-how) as having a life, decision-making power or existence of their own.

This book is written from the point of view of an economist but I am fully aware that there are many behavioural and cognitive questions in this grassroots economic activity that go beyond the scope of this book. We should avoid seeing everything, much less humans, as a machine that is inescapable or that it is escapable only if one loses all social connections that makes one human (Deleuze & Guattari 1983, 1987). My approach aligns more closely with the position or thought stream of Gregory Bateson (1972) who sees humans as able to make mistakes but also able to use technologies in ways that enhance their ability to live in a sustainable and just world. In that sense, the people in grassroots economic initiatives are coordinating themselves to use the technologies, and not the other way around. Whether they achieve their aims or not and how this might be happening is a question of a different order, which the next chapters deal with.

Reproduction of the activity and the people who are involved in it has become my main concern as time has gone by. This is the case because, first, despite any critique about the grassroots economic initiatives, it seems they have huge potential, if not to defy capitalism immediately, at least to educate the people who participate. In addition to that, the communities that are witnesses of the activities learn that there are many other ways of arranging production and distribution of goods and covering human needs than capitalist commodification and exploitation.

Second, because, apart from our individual and collective 're-wiring' of thought, they are experiments where we can easily see what is problematic and resolve it, before taking the activity to a scale that might serve neither its aims nor the people involved in it. What those initiatives do is to really take the generic principle and/or wish of collective decision-making, production and distribution in egalitarian terms, and make it concrete. If we have aspirations to create a better economy, we have to create collective arrangements with specific people, with specific experiences, under specific social constraints and within a specific historical-economic framework that no matter how we want to, will not stop demanding as much as possible of our resources and labour in favour of the mainstream.

Finally, we need to be aware that exactly because it is humans, especially people from the working classes, who participate in those initiatives, the failures of the initiatives or reproduction of injustices will just burden the most vulnerable even more, while they are trying to cope with a political economic system that is against them. Therefore, not paying attention to the challenges that those initiatives face does not serve the people who need those initiatives most.

12

Capitalist patriarchal reprise: Measures and machines as contested means of (re)production

As I have already clarified, the information and discussion presented in the previous chapters do not mean that the economic activity presented in this book is an ideal space of non-patriarchal non-capitalist understandings and practices. It could not be otherwise, given that we all live in capitalist patriarchy and, whether we like it or not, are significantly influenced by it in terms of how we think and how we behave. Actually, it is one of the most difficult questions to tackle when we discuss economic arrangements that try not to be capitalist and hopefully not patriarchal. How is it possible to create ways of practice and ideas that do not reproduce exploitation and injustice in any way?

Neither do I share the view that technologies of any kind are neutral. We would like them to be so, of course. We would like technologies and know-how to be socially impactful only through the type of use one makes of them. Yet, it is normal that the people who construct a technology tend to create what they need, and to search for solutions within the context within which they live. The context, that is, the historical material conditions in which they have to survive, produce, reproduce and collaborate, sets the conditions for what technology will be invented and which technologies out of those invented will be widely used and reproduced. Even the technologies and practices that are found out or invented by mistake or mere serendipity need a certain context, first to be invented, and second, to be perceived as useful so that they are remembered and reproduced.

This context-dependent character of technology means that in societies that are stratified the technologies that are invented are also reflecting the social structure and stratification of those societies. That is, the powerful or/and the rich prefer to have some types of technologies available for them, other types available for the poor and some types of technology are not really acceptable to exist at all. At the same time, those who might be victims of exploitation and suppression are in search and in process of constructing technologies and practices that help them mitigate or eliminate the injustices they face. Their stance towards the technologies that the powerful prefer can be critical or negative altogether. The oppressed might create technologies and practices that they do not talk much about and they prefer to keep going while preserving a low profile for them and their technologies.

In other words, if there are social struggles in a society, those social struggles are also expressed and/or realized through the creation, development, distribution, use, rejection or destruction of technology. This also means that some technological instruments and know-how are created by the poor but are used or even designed by the rich. It means that the elites might want a certain technology to fulfil their purposes. However, what the producers can do while they produce that technology is a major question, linked to work surveillance and monitoring but also to the possibilities the workers have to intervene in the production process. That intervention or design of the technology by the workers might produce something that seems to fulfil the capitalists' aims but also has other twists that one might learn only through the use of the tool (or might never learn, depending on the use people make of it).

To simplify the discussion, let's assume that workers have no ability to twist the technology they create for the capitalists, even if the technology has a vast creative aspect, like the digital technologies have. Let's assume that when a capitalist creates a technology, in reality they have absolute power over the production process and that their employees cannot diverge from any instructions they have received by their managers. In that way, all technology created within this capitalist setting is meant to serve the aims of the capitalists who invested in the technological tools and own them.

Therefore, for analytical purposes only and in order to be able to proceed with our discussion here, let's assume that all digital technologies, in particular those used for information and communication purposes, have been created, developed and disseminated through capitalist patriarchal political economic settings. Let's also assume that because they have been created through those settings, those same technologies are meant to serve only capitalist patriarchy and fulfil the purposes of the capital owners of the early 21st century.

Even if those same technologies, however, have any emancipatory potential, they bear with them extensive histories of exploitation and injustice, which prevent us from seeing them with a light heart and ungrounded optimism. We cannot forget the fact of rare earth extraction and depletion and what this extraction means for the countries where the minerals are located and for their peoples. We cannot forget the slavery-like (or slavery-based) workshops in poor areas of the planet producing and assembling the digital gadgets that capitalists and anti-capitalists use. Irrespective of the use each tool might have at the end of the production and distribution process, the tool itself has been a proof of exploitation and capitalist patriarchy overcoming resistances.

This knowledge is very well disseminated among the people who participate in the grassroots economic schemes. That it is not discussed among the theorists of, for example, parallel currencies, does not mean that the people who use digital technologies to experiment with other transaction modes do not know how their mobiles and computers reach their places. They are very aware of the contradictions related to the technology used and to what they want to achieve concerning economic activity.

Therefore, we cannot assume that any technology that was initially created and massively produced for capitalist profit and/or military purposes was designed to do many more things than the priority aim for which it was conceived. One may use a technology against its main purposes for some time, or for some purposes, especially if the technology has some features that are necessary within a certain context and there is no alternative technological option within that same context. However, one cannot rely on that technology for achieving completely different purposes, unless one redesigns the technology to serve those different purposes (Sotiropoulou 2014b).

Leaving metrical features of digital technology aside, therefore, is a form of grassroots or emergency redesigning of the technology. That is, the necessity to use some technologies for the redesign of which there are not any resources or time, means that the technology will not be fully used. The partial use of a technology within certain contexts is a redesign even if this cannot be a long-term solution.

Moreover, the balanced use of new technologies concerning communication and deliberation shows completely different perceptions from what we usually find in literature about digital cooperative or P2P production. The people participating in the grassroots initiatives mentioned in this book have consciousness about the materiality of their economic activity and economic activity in general. It is not only that they do not abide with theories of 'immaterial labour' and assumptions that with the digital technologies we can establish commons in the virtual world while the tangible commons are ravaged by capitalism. They also understand the materiality of the digital technology itself: an unpaid (obligatorily accounted in official capitalist money) power bill and one might not have internet access; a technical problem and the mobile phone might not be able to function as a communication machine. Let alone the bigger problems of poverty, of public infrastructure that is missing or the environmental impact of digital hardware and of its use.

Beyond the question of the technological tools, there are other aspects of the economic activity that interests us here that are affected by the general context of capitalist patriarchy. Consciousness of materiality does not change the fact that engaging in non-mainstream modes of production and transaction-distribution is not an easy task. It does not change either the fact that a grassroots economic practice is an activity with its own contradictions, irrespective of the technologies a group uses to perform the activity.

We can see three main sets of issues arising for the grassroots economic schemes and their activities.

One set refers to replication of capitalist ideas, perceptions and practices within the initiatives, despite the good intentions of the participants to avoid them. I have already mentioned the problems that the use of the parallel currencies creates when they are pegged to the official currency: prices and valuations of the mainstream (capitalist patriarchal) economy are replicated in the parallel currency scheme. The convenience of 1:1 parity means that people do not practically question the prices they already know in the mainstream economy and just transfer the same or similar prices into the parallel currency scheme. Another problem is the fact that industrial goods are thought to be of great value in the schemes of parallel currency, and they are also well remunerated. This is even more problematic if one takes into account that they are used goods. The people who offer them in great quantities are making income by taking advantage of their class position. At the same time, the food producers have time limitations concerning when they need to have their produce available and for how long (because food has not the durability of clothes, shoes or other industrial goods).

The initiatives that attempt to get industrial goods to be re-used or up-cycled without involving them in monetary transactions are explicitly critical of the social and environmental harms that this industrial production and household accumulation brings. This is why they try to make sure that as many goods as possible are re-used. They are also very strict with people who acquire them for free and then sell them for money. As you may imagine, this type of system abuse is not something that is linked to very low income, to the best of my knowledge based on comments by scheme coordinators. This is why a parallel currency scheme decided to ban used industrial goods from transactions since the beginning of their activity.

Moreover, I question the community role of a parallel currency scheme where used goods could be sold. Before the parallel currency was established, the used items in the same area were shared through regular free bazaars held in public spaces. It seems that the income-generating practice of selling the used goods in the parallel currency markets made the free bazaars redundant. In other words, the parallel currency crowded the free bazaars out as initiatives, because the owners of the used goods were preferring to sell their items. A permanent free bazaar existed in the same area, but the items it contained were well below those offered within the parallel currency scheme for (non-official) money, in terms of both quantity and quality.

In all initiatives, the class position of the people who participate is not easily superseded or hidden. Class is an important factor that defines the chances of each person to participate in the initiative, and much more to cover their needs through it. For example, very low-income people, particularly homeless people or people who live under very dire conditions, might not have any means of production for them to be able to participate in any initiative. The best participation they might be able to perform it is to be receivers in a sharing initiative, like a bazaar, a social kitchen or a social clinic.

Poor people and very poor people, even if they participate in a currency or exchange network, might be forced to receive very low remuneration in order to quickly cover their 'debts' and be able to purchase again what they need in parallel currency. I have seen pressure exerted in public for very low prices in parallel currency on various occasions. In case that pressure is directed towards a very low-income person, it means that this person is cornered economically even in the grassroots initiative, because the grassroots initiative might be their only means of economic survival.

Therefore, participation in exchanging schemes is inhibited even if the schemes themselves and their rules are very open for people with low income. Even if this participation is not inhibited, low-income individuals end up more or less trapped in one more economic situation of underpayment, precarity and absolute poverty (Sotiropoulou 2012c, 2015a). The question of ownership or/and access to means of production is huge and very relevant in this context. It is linked to the possibility of low-income scheme members for truly participating and having some negotiating power is relation to people who have adequate income in the mainstream economy.

The other set of issues stems directly from the patriarchal construction of the economy, and probably would happen with or without the economy being arranged as capitalist. I have already mentioned that food producers continue to receive very low prices compared to prices that used industrial goods receive in a parallel currency scheme. Obviously, in capitalism the disparities between the values of manufactured goods and the values of food produced locally at a small scale have been exacerbated. That happens even if the manufactured goods are second hand.

The devaluation of reproduction labour in patriarchy is fundamental, however. Capitalism built those extreme disparities onto an already existing disdain for farmers, the people who do manual labour and people who work to produce basic necessities, such as food and care work. However, prices are one only way to see this devaluation in grassroots economic schemes.

Generally, patriarchal devaluation of activities such as food production is not only represented in transaction-based initiatives, like currency schemes, but also in schemes where bilateral exchange is not involved at all. For example, the work done in a social kitchen, where food is collectively produced and shared, is not considered to be work. It is also perceived not to have political, especially resistance connotations, when the time comes and the local social movements assess their activity among themselves. That is, the people from the outside the initiative might see the food production and provision as not politically important and as non-work either. The people who work in the kitchen, though, have another perception about it. In particular the women members are very aware of the work/labour character of the activity but also of its importance in terms of political work and resistance practice.

Providing food, therefore, is sometimes considered to be of less importance and less political effectiveness than other forms of resistance that might make the news because mass media prefer fancy photos rather than humble food sharing to be shown to the public. It is not a coincidence that solidarity and generally grassroots initiatives are women dominated. There is always the huge potential created by this active role of women in this type of activity to create economic arrangements for the entire society where capitalist patriarchal practices will not be accepted. But there is also the huge danger of those initiatives becoming one more economic space where the capitalist feminization of poverty and of reproduction labour takes a community twist. I am very happy to report that it is women who defend their work as important and political and do not accept as easily as men the devaluation of the work they do within a solidarity activity (Sotiropoulou 2016a, 2020b). That women are central in this community achievement and have awareness of their own role and the role of the community is something that would need further appreciation and attention in both practice and theory (Edwards 2000, Hossein 2019, Naples 1991).

Another part of those issues stemming from a patriarchal economy is that violence, especially gender-based violence, can erupt and in some cases it can end up being considered normal or expected within a grassroots initiative (Sotiropoulou 2019, 2020b). Most initiatives of all types are very conscious not to allow bad behaviours of any type. Nevertheless, there are initiatives that allow such comportment. In practice, they allow patriarchal violence to establish itself as a mechanism of showing who is working for whom, under which conditions and what types of work the worker is expected to be doing without being able to change those conditions. In those schemes, women, immigrants and people who are facing severe hardship are the easiest targets for very bad behaviours. They might face that behaviour even if they are solidarity workers, that is, they are working for others and their work is absolutely necessary for the scheme to continue its activities.

Violence in those schemes is therefore used in order to command the labour offered, even if the entire structure is cooperative and theoretically there is no need to command any labour. No doubt, there is no need to command labour if you want equality and collective interaction. Yet, there is huge need for the prevailing system and for people who might have any, even slight, privilege in it, to transform the labour offered in egalitarian terms into labour offered under hierarchical and oppressive conditions. Commanding labour and the conditions under which this is offered seems to be necessary for some in order that solidarity workers lose their autonomy and self-confidence to raise issues or defend the importance of their work. It is therefore necessary, if capitalist patriarchy is going to survive or at least discredit the grassroots economic initiatives, to turn them into an appendix of the capitalist patriarchal economic machine by reproducing the same oppressive relationships within the grassroots initiative.

I am not sure how conscious or maximalist the aims are of those who exercise the violence and those who allow it to become systematized, in favour of capitalist patriarchy. They might not understand the harm they do on a collective level. Nevertheless, it is clear they understand the harm they do on an individual level, because they do it only when they know that they will have no real repercussions because of it.

I am not sure either whether the devaluation of some types of labour in general is just a result of our collective economic conditioning or a choice for making sure that reproduction work continues to be offered under unequal terms. If it is the former, then we need to reflect upon how we can un-educate ourselves from that conditioning that makes us see capitalist patriarchal behaviours as normal. If it is the latter, we need to question who in the grassroots schemes gains any benefits on the individual or collective levels from those behaviours. Who is benefiting from a solidarity worker facing sexist behaviours or even violence in the initiatives to which she provides her indispensable labour?

What is important, though, is that other measuring and valuing practices and the use of digital technologies for purposes other than capitalist profit do not on their own create a sheltered economic space where those hierarchies and capitalist patriarchal hierarchies do not exist. There is no direct link or mechanical-linear causality between using other quantity perceptions and machine-use practices and this use automatically making a transaction or sharing egalitarian.

Capitalist measurings and use of technology create inequalities, and non-capitalist measurings are not enough a guarantee for inequalities to be eliminated. Non-capitalist measurings are, however, necessary – at least they could be a good starting point for improving our economies.

Thus, a community can and should use machines and quantification in other ways, but this needs to be combined with other practices to become fully effective. Capitalist patriarchy is an expansive and aggressive economic system that claims resources and labour and punishes all attempts by the working classes to direct resources and labour to other economic arrangements. In that way, capitalist patriarchy makes sure that the community work that the grassroots initiatives represent is erased. Or, this community work is often expected to be co-opted by capitalism as a good and cheap way of keeping people alive to be 'used', if needed, after the restructuring of the economy, at their own expense and not at the expense of capital(ists).

I am not sharing the view that the aims and co-option ability of capitalist patriarchy (especially of patriarchy) determine on their own the route a grassroots initiative might take. This also makes me very wary of the fact that other ways of measuring and machine-using can also become ways of exploitation that existed before or in parallel with capitalism. This is something that participants, in particular the older ones, pointed out to me from time to time. The use of non-monetary transactions for exploitation is a practice that has a long history in Greece and people have awareness of the tricky character of flat statements about non-monetary exchanges and money. There are many ways whereby injustice, exploitation and hierarchy might enter an economic arrangement. Avoiding the capitalist patriarchal traps is just one, although major, part of the effort undertaken by the people who engage in non-mainstream modes of transaction and production (Sotiropoulou 2013).

The third set of issues are those that would exist even if, in some way, capitalism and patriarchy disappeared all of sudden, both from our economic activity and from our ways of thinking and acting. For example, if someone goes to a free bazaar and sweeps up most of the items, or most of that which is in good condition, this behaviour in reality prevents other people from covering their needs. The same behaviour becomes even more problematic if it happens, for example, in a social kitchen. If someone sweeps one of the shelves of packs of food (like pasta, rice, beans) that were meant to be cooked for the next week, it will create a huge problem for all the people of the initiative, both those who receive the food and those who were assigned to cook it.

In those cases, the problem, as defined by the participants of the initiatives, is not that someone takes without giving back. There is no problem either if someone takes without asking for permission or for an arrangement if that person has some reason to take some supposedly common things.

The problem is quantity itself: it has been clear in discussions and assemblies discussing incidents of this type, that it is understandable that someone feels embarrassed to ask for more things to take and takes the liberty to grab a pack of pasta to cook at home. However, taking all pasta available without deliberation with the group means that one is not in need for one day or two but one is storing food at the expense of the daily meal of many other people. The people who miss their meal might be in the same bad condition as the person who took too many food items. In many cases, people who participate in a bazaar or social kitchen or social clinic might ask for less than what they need because they do not want to burden the initiative or the other people who also need something. The person who is sweeping vast numbers of items that everyone needs goes against this stance of sharing and respect of the needs of others.

Those incidents of massive appropriation have a completely different quality from appropriating the absolutely necessary. Massive appropriation is something that, although it exists in both capitalist and other forms of patriarchy, can still happen in a very communal non-patriarchal setting.

It is very important to note, as mentioned before, that digitization was never mentioned in any discussion as a way of controlling this type of appropriation. Even in such problematic situations, measuring continued to be done 'in approximation'. The aim has always been to make sure that the majority of people, who anyway would never appropriate at the expense of others, feel free to do what they need to do, even if this is to take some more stuff from the bazaar or the solidarity initiative.

From the above it is evident that people who participate in grassroots economic activity and use digital technologies for their ends are highly aware that 'the revolution will not be automated' but it will be well grounded in social relations and material conditions that communities are facing (Khoo 2018, Mostafa 2019). Using machines otherwise or using them moderately in combination with other quantification approaches has a lot of issues to resolve, exactly because it is not only capitalism and not only patriarchy that might make a community arrangement ineffective or working at the expense of the most disadvantaged. Nevertheless, even this revelation of contradictions and the attempt to resolve them in practice seems to create some potential for further social and economic exploration that the use of machines and measures in the mainstream economy does not seem to allow.

13

Conclusion: 'The master's tools will never dismantle the master's house' and the options we have

As you may imagine, I agree with Audre Lorde's statement (1979). For this reason, all efforts to construct technologies and measuring practices that are the tools of free people and free communities who live in harmony with nature and in justice among themselves, always have my support and admiration. For this same reason, I study and (try to) think with a critical stance about all practices that are aspiring to be non-capitalist and non-patriarchal. The last thing we need is to replace the existing patriarchy with an upgraded one, that will have as a cover the 'non-capitalist' or the 'alternative' banner.

However, as we have seen in the previous chapters, there is a great deal of complexity in the discussion about tools. The complexity is even more extensive concerning the sophisticated tools that are representing quantities or are handling vast amounts of information, like the digital technologies do. We have seen that in some cases, people in grassroots initiatives do not use the mainstream tools, whether those are measures or digital gadgets. In other cases, we saw them twist or redesign the tools' use for their own purposes, as is done in time banks or in social kitchens. We have seen problems that emerge if a community uses a quantification or accounting instrument that has strong connections or similarities to accounting instruments that the prevailing economic system uses, such as what has happened with parallel currencies. And we have also seen that there are challenges that arise in grassroots economic activity that are linked to capitalist patriarchal injustices despite the fact that the schemes might have a clearly non-monetary or even straightforward sharing and solidarity character.

There is much discussion about the history of the tools, in particular the history of quantity and measures. Just like with technologies that are quite old or ancient, there is a debate whether those tools were really created by or in order to serve an exploitative system or structure like the patriarchal economic system. Or we would need to debate whether those same tools were constructed initially for other purposes and have been appropriated for so long for the purpose of economic exploitation that their initial character has been forgotten. It could be a possibility that their function was so much altered that we cannot even imagine them to serve an egalitarian society without masters and exploitation.

This is, no doubt, a discussion that goes beyond the scope of this book. It is useful to remember, however, that at any point it is the specific material, historical context and the conditions of the economic activity that define a great deal about the role of a quantity perception or measurement tool in each specific case. We need to be aware at any moment whether a tool is really a tool created by or under the control of a master; and if this is the case, and if the tool cannot be replaced by a better one at a certain point of time, whether this tool can be used temporarily and under certain restrictions for purposes other than what the master wanted the tool to be used for.

Nevertheless, the quest for ensuring that the production and sharing we need in our communities is done to as great an extent as possible away from the capitalist patriarchal settings and hierarchies has long ago taken a character of great urgency. We need to explore how to support the reproduction of nature, of ourselves as human beings and of our communities within frameworks of increasing capitalist patriarchal restructuring and aggressiveness. Reproduction emerges as the main question for all economic activity, but particularly about quantification and machine use as tools of that activity (Weiner 1980).

We need to always think and invent means of reproduction of our communities and nature that are fit for collective emancipatory justice-oriented purposes. We know that exploitation and oppression exist exactly so that most people are not able to invent or even use any such means of reproduction. We cannot say that because a social clinic is using a website or digital register for their medicine stock, the entire initiative is already defeated. It could be defeated, but this contradiction alone is not enough for us to proceed with such a judgement.

Just like we question the social clinic for using digital technologies, we need to question what would happen if they did not use those technologies. We need to investigate if the people who need healthcare and those who generously work to provide it had other options; or whether the website was their only effective option to become accessible to the public but also to protect the activity itself (in some cases, the grassroots initiatives receive overt or covert repression by the state authorities).

The same is the case with the use of quantities and measures: other quantities are necessary, while other quantities are not necessary to use in our economic activities. 'Necessary for whom and for what purpose?' appears to be a useful criterion for understanding the implications of each practice.

After all, we cannot criticize the oppressed for trying to save their lives, their livelihoods and their communities by using any means that are available to them – while they do not do it at the expense of other people who are more oppressed than them. It is not a critique either. It is the recognition that technologies, whether digital or social (like quantities and measures) tend to fulfil their core design purposes more than anything else. A hammer tends to hit nails even if one wants to use it for painting.

As a researcher I would plead here for more investigation and research concerning quantities, measures and valuation processes that are not promoting patriarchy and capitalism. I cherish the critique we have about those tools in capitalism, because without that critique we would not be able to understand how those 'master's tools' are used against us and how they can lurk in our collective efforts to divert them to reproduce 'the master's house'. Yet, we need more knowledge than that and this can only be done in a collective manner.

As a person who fully supports all grassroots economic arrangements that are against exploitation, injustice, racism and nature's degradation, I also want to see communities' and grassroots' collective efforts to take over the knowledge production and evaluation process. They do already, in the sense that they produce and choose to develop original knowledge irrespective of whether people in academia or theorists put it on digital or print paper or not. Learning and understanding those economic activities through the knowledge and approaches that make them possible is absolutely necessary in order to avoid imposing capitalist patriarchal understandings on activities that aspire to be better than the existing economic system (Hossein 2019).

This knowledge has been and will always be a collective creation no matter what capitalist patriarchy thinks it can do or attempts to do with it. We need the research I mentioned above to be done with the communities leading in the design, priorities, questions and debates. The ones who write books like this one, might have good intentions but cannot replace a community.

Personally, I would never want to. My intention has been to share what various communities have taught me and also to show that we need not despair. There are ways to supersede the impasses we are trapped in, both practically but also in terms of thinking. Because there are so many possibilities, it is impossible not to find at least one, or at least several other pathways for economic organizing.

Notes

Chapter 5

1   Cooperatives are not included in this book, because they are both legal entities according to official laws, and use official currency in their work. There is a vast amount of unpaid work and non-monetary arrangements in cooperatives too, but the main aspect of their activity remains connected to the mainstream economy. They would require a separate study to be analysed with respect to the use of measurement methods and digital machinery.

2   The discussion was lurking in the schemes in a very informal and private way since 2009 when they started being established. However, in the Pan-Hellenic PhD Workshop-Conference 'Issues of Research Methodology in Social Sciences', held in Rethymno, at the University of Crete (26–28 October 2012), a specially themed thread of sessions on Social & Solidarity Economy was held. On Saturday 27 October 2012 the representatives of the grassroots initiatives who had the floor for the morning sessions mentioned for the first time in public that the prices of the mainstream economy are transferred to the parallel currency initiatives due to the association of the parallel currency to the euro.

3   Being economically active and trying to survive when having a low income in an economy with multiple currencies circulating is not a new experience for the people who live in Greece. Actually, even in the 1980s and while the official currency (drachma) was under severe inflation, US dollars, regular pounds sterling and golden British pounds, along with Deutschemarks were circulating in the Greek market extensively, even if the law prohibited transactions in currencies other than the drachma. The circulation of multiple currencies has been common during the history of the Greek state (established in 1830) and before that during the Ottoman, Venetian and Byzantine rules of the country or parts of it.

4   Some people have their own weight scales when they make exchanges. It is interesting to note that they do not check whether their statements understate the quantity they give to other people, but they are very alert

to avoiding overstating quantity. This suggests that some measurement takes place on their part to make sure that they never give less than stated, and then they add more quantity without measuring it. In my research, when I was doing random checks, I was using the scales of the participants. It was obvious that everyone had weighted the products to make sure they were not less than stated, and in most cases the over-weight/volume was significantly greater than the stated amount of product offered by the producers. The producers were very happy that someone was showcasing that they were offering more, because they would never boast about it themselves. This also shows that everyone knew but the generous measures are both generous and silent.

Chapter 8

1   Refugees did not start coming to Greece or passing through Greece aiming to reach Northern Central or Western Europe in 2015, but well in advance of that year. They continue to be forced to migrate and they come to or pass through Greece, although it seems that their stories are no longer fashionable or interesting for mass media to be featured in regular reports. The refugees' needs have not diminished and many of them have been trapped in Greece, in detention centres and refugee camps, with no adequate food, medical care, shelter, hygiene or heating. However, 2015 was a turning point in terms of the numbers of people who had to forcibly migrate to Europe, and also in terms of how those people had to pass to Northern Europe on foot. They were not allowed to travel by any transport means, and in many cases, they were not even allowed to proceed on foot through the borders of Greece, Eastern European countries Italy and Austria and other Central European countries. Well before 2015, people in Greece took a stance to help, and they continue to do so – while on the other hand the official state policies are both opposed to refugees and tolerant of racist and Nazi attacks on refugees by some members of the local population. The mobilization that took place in 2015 was unprecedented in the modern history of the country in terms of resources, work, organizing, management and lack of

formal organizational support by any political parties or formal organizations, which proved unable both to anticipate the extent of the continuous needs and the work those needed to be covered. When NGOs and the European states started to be involved with supporting refugees, the vast number of them were already on the routes to Northern Europe, having survived by grassroots support in Greece and in many other countries and despite all of the violence they faced from institutional and non-institutional racism in those same countries. To my view, the role of the internet in organizing the support in material terms and in a decentralized but effective way was instrumental.

Chapter 11

1   It is a huge question how and why some initiatives are more mixed in terms of origin of people and some are not. I associate the differences in the structure of each initiative – well linked to the quantification each activity entails. For example, it is more common to see an active policy to translate main documents and announcements into several languages other than Greek in initiatives such as free bazaars and solidarity initiatives such as social kitchens, social clinics or social educational institutes rather than in parallel currencies. To the best of my knowledge, only one currency scheme had announcements in various languages from the very beginning. It is also obvious that the rules of each activity prevent many people with other cultural backgrounds from participating. For example, the people who are unemployed immigrants, and in danger of being arrested by the police for expired residence permit, cannot practically register with a parallel currency, even if they want to. They can, however, participate in a bazaar or collective cultivation or a social kitchen, where registration is not needed, and their skills can be invaluable as they are also cultural and/or community mediators between the local people and the people who are from the same culture as them. These solidarity workers are able to facilitate access to the activity as production space and socializing opportunity to many people who otherwise would not be able to participate.

Bibliography

Ackerman F. & Heinzerling L. (2001). Pricing the priceless: Cost-benefit analysis of environmental protection. *University of Pennsylvania Law Review*, 150, 1553–84.

Adkins L. (2009). Feminism after measure. *Feminist Theory*, 10(3), 323–39.

Agathangelou A. M. & Ling L. H. M. (2006). *Fear and property: Why a liberal social ontology fails postcolonial states*. International Affairs Working Paper 2006–07. Paper for a panel on 'Contesting modern state: Stateness in the postcolonial world', International Studies Association, 22–26 March 2006, San Diego, California.

Albritton R. (2003). Marx's value theory and subjectivity. In Westra R. & Zuege A. (eds), *Value and the world economy today: Production, finance and globalization*. Palgrave Macmillan, 205–24.

Anagnostopoulos A. & Siebert S. (2015). The impact of Greek labour market regulation on temporary employment: Evidence from a survey in Thessaly, Greece. *The International Journal of Human Resource Management*, 26(18), 2366–93.

Apostolopoulou E. & Adams W. M. (2015). Neoliberal capitalism and conservation in the post-crisis era: The dialectics of 'green' and 'un-green' grabbing in Greece and the UK. *Antipode*, 47(1), 15–35.

Applin S. (2017). The automation and privatization of community knowledge. *Savage Minds: Notes and Queries in Anthropology*, 1 October. Last accessed on 18 October 2022, https://savageminds.org/2017/10/01/the-automation-and-privatization-of-community-knowledge/

Arjaliès D. L. & Bansal P. (2018). Beyond numbers: How investment managers accommodate societal issues in financial decisions. *Organization Studies*, 39(5–6), 691–719.

Arntz M., Gregory T. & Zierahn U. (2016). *The risk of automation for jobs in OECD countries: A comparative analysis*. OECD Social, Employment & Migration Working Papers no 189. DELSA/ELSA/WD/SEM(2016)15.

Automating Banishment (2021). *The surveillance and policing of looted lands*. Community-based report, Land & Policing Workshop, November.

Barker D. K. & Feiner S. F. (2010). As the world turns: Globalization, consumption, and the feminization of work. *Rethinking Marxism: A Journal of Economics, Culture & Society*, 22(2), 246–52.

Barker D. K. & Kuiper E. (eds) (2003). *Toward a feminist philosophy of economics*. Routledge.

Bastani A. (2019). *Fully automated luxury communism*. Verso Books.

Bateson G. (1972). *Steps to an ecology of mind (A revolutionary approach to man's understanding of himself)*. Ballantine Books.

Beer D. (2016). *Metric power*. Palgrave Macmillan.

Bennholdt-Thomsen V., Mies M. & Von Werlhof C. (1988). *Women: The last colony*. Zed Books.

Berdayes V. (2002). Traditional management theory as panoptic discourse: Language and the constitution of somatic flows. *Culture and Organization*, 8(1), 35–49.

Berend I. T. (2005). Foucault and the welfare state. *European Review*, 13, 551–56.

Berman E. P. & Hirschman D. (2018). The sociology of quantification: Where are we now? *Contemporary Sociology*, 47(3), 257–66.

Bey, M. (2021). *Black trans feminism*. Duke University Press.

Borneman E. (1975). *Das Patriarchat, Ursprung und Zukunft unseres Gesellschafts systems*. Fischer Taschenbuch Verlag.

Borneman E. (1979). *Le Patriarcat*. Presses universitaires de France.

Boumans M. (2005). Measurement in economic systems. *Measurement*, 38(4), 275–84.

Boumans M. (ed.) (2007). *Measurement in economics: A handbook*. Elsevier.

Bruno I., Didier E. & Vitale T. (2014). Statactivism: Forms of action between disclosure and affirmation. *Partecipazione e conflitto – The Open Journal of Sociopolitical Studies*, 16(7, 2), 198–220.

Cabot H. (2016). 'Contagious' solidarity: Reconfiguring care and citizenship in Greece's social clinics. *Social Anthropology* 24(2), 152–66.

Caffentzis G. (2002). On the notion of a crisis of social reproduction: A theoretical review. *The Commoner*, 5, 1–22.

Campbell M. (2005). Marx's explanation of money's functions: Overturning the quantity theory. In Moseley F. (ed.), *Marx's theory of money*. Palgrave Macmillan, 143–59.

Cassano G. (ed.). (2009). *Class struggle on the home front: Work, conflict, and exploitation in the household*. Springer.

Chandler D. & Fuchs C. (eds) (2019). *Digital objects, digital subjects: Interdisciplinary perspectives on capitalism, labour and politics in the age of big data*. University of Westminster Press.

Charmaz K. (2006). *Constructing grounded theory: A practical guide through qualitative analysis*. SAGE.

Cheng E., Wang G. & Zhu K. (2019). *The creation of value by living labour: A normative and empirical study*, vol 1. Trans. Hui Lui and Sun Yexia; translating eds Alan Freeman and Sun Yexia. Canut International Publishers.

Cole M. (2018). Automation. https://autonomy.work/. Last accessed on 8 September 2018 (page no longer live, pdf in author's files).

Courville C. (1993 (2005)). Re-examining patriarchy as a mode of production. In James S. M. & Busia A. P. A. (eds), *Theorizing black feminisms: The visionary pragmatism of black women*. Routledge, 31–44.

Cowton C. J. & Dopson S. (2002). Foucault's prison? Management control in an automotive distributor. *Management Accounting Research*, 13(2), 191–213.

Crosby A. W. (1998). *The measure of reality: Quantification in Western Europe, 1250-1600*. Cambridge University Press.

Dalla Costa M. & James S. (1975). *The power of women and the subversion of the community*. Falling Wall Press and individuals from Women's Movement in England and Italy.

Daskalaki M., Fotaki M. & Sotiropoulou I. (2018). Performing values practices and grassroots organizing: The case of solidarity economy initiatives in Greece. *Organization Studies*, Online first, 1–25.

Davis A. (2011). *Women, race, & class*. Vintage Books.

Deleuze G. & Guattari F. (1983). *Anti-Oedipus: Capitalism and schizophrenia*. Trans. R. Hurley, M. Seem & H. R. Lane. University of Minnesota Press.

Deleuze G. & Guattari F. (1987). *A thousand plateaus: Capitalism and schizophrenia*. Trans. B. Massumi. University of Minnesota Press.

Demsetz H. (1964). The exchange and enforcement of property rights. *Journal of Law and Economics*, 7 (October), 11–26.

Diamond P. A. & Hausman J. A. (1994). Contingent valuation: Is some number better than no number? *Journal of Economic Perspectives*, 8(4), 45–64.

Diaz-Bone R. & Didier E. (2016). Introduction: The sociology of quantification – perspectives on an emerging field in the social sciences. *Historical Social Research/Historische Sozialforschung*, 7–26.

Dorrestijn S. (2012). Technical mediation and subjectivation: Tracing and extending Foucault's philosophy of technology. *Philosophy & Technology*, 25(2), 221–41.

Duncan O. D. (1984). *Notes on social measurement: Historical and critical.* Russell Sage Foundation.

Dutta S. & Mia I. (2009). *The Global Information Technology Report 2008–2009 – Mobility in a networked world.* World Economic Forum & INSEAD.

Dyer-Witherford N. (2013). Red Plenty Platforms. *Culture Machine*, 14, 1–27.

Edwards A. E. (2000). Community mothering: The relationship between mothering and community work of black women. *Journal of the Association for Research on Mothering*, 2(2), 88–100.

Ehrenreich B. (2002). *Nickel and dimed: Undercover in low-wage USA.* Granta Books.

Ehrenreich B. & English D. (1973). *Witches, midwives and nurses: A history of women healers.* Feminist Press. (Also available at: https://www.marxists. org/subject/women/authors/ehrenreich-barbara/witches.htm, last accessed on 18 October 2022.)

Ehrenreich B. & English D. ([1978] 2005). *For her own good.* Anchor Books.

Eisenstein Z. (1979). *Capitalist patriarchy and the case for socialist feminism.* Monthly Review Press.

Emmanuel A. (1976). The "stabilization" alibi of international exploitation (La "stabilisation" alibi de l' exploitation internationale). Revue Tiers Monde, 17(66), 257–264.

Espeland W. N. & Stevens M. L. (2008). A sociology of quantification. *European Journal of Sociology/Archives Européennes de Sociologie*, 49(3), 401–36.

Espeland W. N. & Vannebo B. I. (2007). Accountability, quantification, and law. *Annual Review of Law and Social Science*, 3, 21–43.

Featherstone K. (2005). 'Soft' co-ordination meets 'hard' politics: The European Union and pension reform in Greece. *Journal of European Public Policy*, 12(4), 733–50.

Federici S. (2004). *Caliban and the witch.* Autonomedia.

Federici S. (2013). *Revolucion en punto cero: Trabajo domestico, reproduccion y luchas feministas.* Trans. Scriptorium (C. Fernandez-Cuervos and P. Martin-Ponz). Traficantes de Sueños-Mapas.

Foucault M. (1988). *Madness and civilization: A history of insanity in the age of reason.* Vintage Books.

Foucault M. (1995). *Discipline and punish: The birth of the prison.* Trans. A. Sheridan. Vintage Books.

Foucault M. & Simon J. K. (1991). Michel Foucault on Attica: An interview. *Social Justice*, 18(3) (45), 26–34.

Fraser N. (2013a). *Fortunes of feminism: From state-managed capitalism to neoliberal crisis.* Verso Books.

Fraser N. (2013b). How feminism became capitalism's handmaiden – and how to reclaim it. *The Guardian*, 14 October. Last accessed on 18 October 2022, https://www.theguardian.com/commentisfree/2013/oct/14/feminism-capitalist-handmaiden-neoliberal

Gemmill E. & Mayhew N. (1995). *Changing values in medieval Scotland: A study of prices, money and weights and measures.* Cambridge University Press.

Georgakopoulos S. (2021). Greece: 'Police everywhere, doctors nowhere' (Ελλάδα: «Παντού αστυνομικοί, πουθενά γιατροί»). Deutsche Welle online, 5 February. Last accessed on 18 October 2022, www.dw.com/el/ελλάδα-παντού-αστυνομικοί-πουθενά-γιατροί/a-56461646.

Giblin R. & Doctorow C. (2022). *Chokepoint capitalism: How big tech and big content captured creative labor markets and how we'll win them back.* Beacon Press.

Gibson-Graham J. K. (2006). *A postcapitalist politics.* University of Minnesota Press.

Giniger N. & Sotiropoulou I. (2019). 'Less state' in austerity: A concept masking the central agent of neoliberal policies. In Ali T., Power K. & Lebduskova E. (eds), *Discourse analysis and austerity: Critical studies from economics and linguistics.* Routledge Frontiers of Political Economy, 80–107.

Glaser B. G. and Strauss A. L. ([1967] 2006). *The discovery of grounded theory: Strategies for qualitative research.* Aldine Transaction Publishers.

Glenn J. G. (2019). *Foucault and post-financial crises: Governmentality, discipline and resistance.* Palgrave Macmillan.

Graeber D. (2006). Turning modes of production inside out: Or, why capitalism is a transformation of slavery. *Critique of Anthropology*, 26(1), 61–85.

Graeber D. (2011). *Debt: The first 5000 years.* Melville House Publishing.

Graeber D. (2018). *Bullshit jobs: A theory.* Simon & Schuster.

Hadjimichalis C. & Vaiou D. (1990). Flexible labour markets and regional development in northern Greece. *International Journal of Urban and Regional Research*, 14(1), 1–24.

hooks b. (1984). *Feminist theory: From margin to center.* South End Press.

hooks b. (1997). *Cultural criticism and transformation.* Interview transcript, produced by Sut Jhally. Media Education Foundation.

Hopper T. & Macintosh N. (1998). Management accounting numbers: Freedom or prison – Geneen versus Foucault. In McKinlay A. &

Starkey K. (eds), *Foucault, management and organization theory: From panopticon to technologies of self.* SAGE Publications, 126–50.

Hossein C. S. (2019). A black epistemology for the social and solidarity economy: The black social economy. *The Review of Black Social Economy*, 46(3), 209–29.

Hull G. (2015). Successful failure: What Foucault can teach us about privacy self-management in a world of Facebook and big data. *Ethics and Information Technology*, 17(2), 89–101.

Kapitsinis N. (2022). The 2007/08 capitalist crisis evolution in Greece: A geographical political economy perspective. *Human Geography*, 19427786221096873.

Karaliotas L. (2017). Performing neoliberalization through urban infrastructure: Twenty years of privatization policies around Thessaloniki's port. *Environment and Planning A*, 49(7), 1556–74.

Karanikolos M., Kentikelenis A., McKee M., Reeves A. & Stuckler D. (2014). Greece's health crisis: From austerity to denialism. *Lancet*, 383(9918), 748–53.

Khoo C. (2018). The revolution will not be automated: Asserting a place for labour within the technosocial gestalt. Canadian Centre for Policy Alternatives, 1 July. Last accessed on 18 October 2022, https://policyalternatives.ca/publications/monitor/revolution-will-not-be-automated

Koratzanis N. & Pierros C. (2017). Assessing the impact of austerity in the Greek economy: A sectoral financial balances approach. *Real World Economics Review*, 82, 122–42.

Kurz R. (2014). The crisis of exchange value: Science as productive force, productive labor and capitalist reproduction. In Brown N., Larsen N., Nilgcn M. & Robinson J. (eds), *Marxism and the critique of value.* M-C-M' Publishing, 17–76.

Labatut J., Aggeri F. & Girard, N. (2011). Discipline and change: How technologies and organizational routines interact in new practice. *Organization Studies*, 33(1), 39–69.

Lanier J. (2018). *Ten arguments for deleting your social media accounts right now.* Random House.

Large J. (2018). The future of work, automation and the left. *Notes from Below*, Technology and The Worker (#2), 30 March. Last accessed on 18 October 2022, https://notesfrombelow.org/article/the-future-of-work

Lau K. C. (2020). Revisiting collectivism and rural governance in China: The singularity of the Zhoujiazhuang People's Commune. *Monthly Review: An independent socialist magazine*, 72, 35–49.

Lave J. (1984). The values of quantification. *The Sociological Review*, 32(S1), 88–111.

Lazzarato M. (2011). *The fabrication of the indebted man: Essay on the neoliberal condition (La fabrique de l'homme endetté: Essai sur la condition néolibérale)*. Amsterdam.

Lerner G. (1986). *The creation of patriarchy*, vol. 1. Oxford Paperbacks.

Likitkijsomboon P. (2005). Marx's anti-quantity theory of money: A critical evaluation. In Moseley F. (ed.), *Marx's theory of money*. Palgrave Macmillan, 160–74.

Lohmann L. (2020). *Blockchain machines, earth beings and the labour of trust*. The Corner House. Last accessed on 18 October 2022, https://www. wrongkindofgreen.org/wp-content/uploads/2020/04/BLOCKCHAIN-MACHINES-EARTH-BEINGS-AND-THE-LABOUR-OF-TRUST-LOHMANN.pdf

Lorde A. (1979). Comments during 'The Personal and the Political Panel', Second Sex Conference, New York, September 29, 1979. (Also available as Lorde A. (1984). 'The master's tools will never dismantle the master's house', in *Sister outsider*. Crossing Press, 110–13.)

Lytras T. (2022). Healthcare system overstretch and in-hospital mortality of intubated COVID-19 patients in Greece: an updated analysis, September 2020 to April 2022. Manuscript preprint. Last accessed on 28 November 2022 at https://europepmc.org/article/ppr/ppr550414

Lytras T & Tsiodras S. (2022). Total patient load, regional disparities and in-hospital mortality of intubated COVID-19 patients in Greece, from September 2020 to May 2021. Scandinavian Journal of Public Health, 50(6), 671–75.

Maris G. & Flouros F. (2022). Economic crisis, COVID-19 pandemic, and the Greek model of capitalism. *Evolutionary and Institutional Economics Review*, 19(1), 469–84.

Marx K. (1992). *Capital*, vols 1–3: *A critique of political economy*. Penguin.

Mayer-Schönberger V. & Cukier K. (2013). *Big data: A revolution that will transform how we live, work, and think*. Houghton Mifflin Harcourt.

Mayer-Schönberger V. and Ramge T. (2018). *Reinventing capitalism in the age of big data*. Hachette UK.

Mayes E. (2005). Private property, the private subject and women: Can women truly be owners of capital? In Albertson Fineman M. & Dougherty T. (eds), *Feminism confronts homo economicus: Gender, law and society.* Cornell University Press, 117–28.

McKinlay A. & Pezet E. (2010). Accounting for Foucault. *Critical Perspectives on Accounting*, 21(6), 486–95.

Mcm_cmc (2015). Fully automated luxury communism: A utopian critique. Libcom.org 14 June. Last accessed on 18 October 2022, https://libcom.org/article/fully-automated-luxury-communism-utopian-critique

McNamee R. (2020). *Zucked: Waking up to the Facebook catastrophe.* Penguin Press.

Meikle S. (2000). Quality and quantity in economics: The metaphysical construction of the economic realm. *New Literary History*, 31(2), 247–68.

Mennicken A. & Nelson Espeland W. (2019). What's new with numbers? Sociological approaches to the study of quantification. *Annual Review of Sociology*, 45, 223–45.

Mennicken A. & Salais R. (eds) (2022). *The new politics of numbers: Utopia, evidence and democracy.* Palgrave Macmillan.

Mies M. (1998). *Patriarchy and accumulation on a world scale: Women in the international division of labour.* Palgrave Macmillan.

Mies M. & Shiva V. (1993). *Ecofeminism.* Zed Books.

Mirowski P. & Nik-Khah E. (2017). *The knowledge we have lost in information: The history of information in modern economics.* Oxford University Press.

Moore P. (2011). FCJ-119 Subjectivity in the ecologies of P2P production. *The Fibreculture Journal* (17).

Moore P. V. & Robinson A. (2016). The quantified self: What counts in the neoliberal workplace. *New Media and Society*, 18(11), 2774–92.

Moore P. V., Upchurch M. & Whittaker X. (eds) (2018). *Humans and machines at work.* Palgrave Macmillan.

Morozov E. (2013). *To save everything, click here: The folly of technological solutionism.* Public Affairs.

Morozov E. & Bria F. (2018). *Rethinking the smart city: Democratizing urban technology.* Rosa Luxemburg Stiftung.

Morozov E. (2019). Digital socialism? The calculation debate in the age of big data. *New Left Review* 116/117 (March–June). Last accessed on 18 October 2022, https://newleftreview.org/issues/ii116/articles/evgeny-morozov-digital-socialism

Mostafa J. (2019). The revolution will not be automated (Review of Shoshana Zuboff and Aaron Bastani's books). *Sydney Review of Books*, 23 July. Last accessed on 18 October 2022, https://sydneyreviewofbooks.com/review/zuboff-bastani/

Muller J. Z. (2018). *The tyranny of metrics*. Princeton University Press.

Mundell R. (1961). A theory of optimum currency areas. *The American Economic Review*, 51(4), 657–65.

Naples N. A. (1991). 'Just what needed to be done': The political practice of women community workers in low-income neighborhoods. *Gender & Society* 5(4), 479–94.

Nembhard J. G. (2014). *Collective courage: A history of African American economic thought and practice*. The Pennsylvania State University Press.

Nembhard J. G. & Ifateyo A. N. (2014). Black co-ops were a method of economic survival: An interview with Prof. J. G. Nembhard. Grassroots Economic Organizing, 27 May. Last accessed on 18 October 2022, https://geo.coop/story/black-co-ops-were-method-economic-survival

Newton T. (1998). Theorizing subjectivity in organizations: The failure of Foucauldian studies? *Organization Studies*, 19(3), 415–47.

Ntouka N. (2010). The problem with the diabetic patients' shoes was finally resolved – Social Insurance Institute will cover the expenses (Λύθηκε τελικά το πρόβλημα με τα παπούτσια των διαβητικών - Θα τα καλύπτει το ΙΚΑ). Last accessed on 18 October 2022, https://www.thebest.gr/article/34847-

O'Neil C. (2016). *Weapons of math destruction: How big data increases inequality and threatens democracy*. Broadway Books.

O'Neill C. (2016/2017). Taylorism, the European science of work, and the quantified self at work. *Science, Technology, & Human Values*, 42(4), 600–21.

Pagones J. (2013). The European Union's response to the sovereign debt crisis: Its effect on labor relations in Greece. *Fordham International Law Review*, 36(5), 1517–54.

Pempetzoglou Z. & Patergiannaki M. (2017). Debt-driven water privatization: The case of Greece. *European Journal of Multidisciplinary Studies*, 2(5), 102–11.

Peterson V. S. (2003). *A critical rewriting of global political economy: Integrating reproductive, productive, and virtual economies*. Psychology Press.

Peterson V. S. (2010). A long view of globalization and crisis. *Globalizations*, 7(1–2), 187–202.

Peterson V. S. (1997). Whose crisis? Early and post-modern masculinism. In Gill S. & Mittelman J. H. (eds), *Innovation and transformation in International Studies*. Cambridge University Press, 185–202.

Petit C. (2015). L'avènement de la société de prédation, conséquence du remplacement du travail de l'homme par la machine (The advent of the predatory society, a consequence of the replacement of human labor by the machine). *Journal du MAUSS – Mouvement Anti-Utilitariste dans les Sciences Sociales*, 7 March. Last accessed on 18 October 2022, https://www.journaldumauss.net/?L-avenement-de-la-societe-de-1217

Picchio A. (ed.) (2005). *Unpaid work and the economy: A gender analysis of the standards of living*. Routledge.

Porter T. M. (2012). Funny numbers. *Culture Unbound*, 4(4), 585–98.

Porter T. M. (1995). *Trust in numbers: The pursuit of objectivity in science and public life*. Princeton University Press.

Revoy B. (1998). Jevons on measurement. Replay: The mathematisation of economics in the Jevonsonian theory. *Recherches Économiques de Louvain/ Louvain Economic Review*, 64(3), 353–6.

Robinson C. J. (2000). *Black Marxism: The making of the black radical tradition*. Revised and updated third edition. The University of North Carolina Press.

Rodney W. (1981). *How Europe underdeveloped Africa*. Howard University Press.

Rogobete S. E. (2015). The self, technology and the order of things: In dialogue with Heidegger, Ellul, Foucault and Taylor. *Procedia-Social and Behavioral Sciences*, 183, 122–8.

Saltelli A. (2020). Ethics of quantification or quantification of ethics? *Futures*, 116, 102509.

Saltelli A., Bammer G., Bruno I., Charters E., Di Fiore M., Didier E., Espeland W. N., Kay J., Piano S. L., Mayo D. & Pielke Jr, R. (2020). Five ways to make models serve society: A manifesto. *Nature* 582, supplementary online material.

Saros D. E. (2014). *Information technology and socialist construction: The end of capital and the transition to socialism*. Routledge.

Sawicki J. (1987). Heidegger and Foucault: Escaping technological nihilism. *Philosophy & Social Criticism*, 13(2), 155–73.

Scholz R. (2014). Patriarchy and commodity society: Gender without the body. In Brown N., Larsen N., Nilgen M. & Robinson J. (eds), *Marxism and the critique of value*. M-C-M' Publishing, 123–42.

Schrift A. D. (2013). Discipline and punish. In Falzon C., O'Leary T. & Sawicki J. (eds), *A companion to Foucault*. Wiley-Blackwell, 137–53.

Schumacher E. F. (2011). Small is beautiful: A study of economics as if people mattered. Random House.

Sotiropoulou I. (2011a). How environmental awareness can be practical and funny while puzzling economists: Exchange networks, parallel currencies & free bazaars in Greece. *Journal of Innovation Economics*, 2(8), 89–117.

Sotiropoulou I. (2011b). Transactions without euro in times of crisis: Coincidence, affinity or challenge? 'Europe and Greece beyond the Economic Crisis' conference, Messolonghi, Greece, 10–11 November. Technological Institute of Messolonghi.

Sotiropoulou I. (2012a). Exchange networks and parallel currencies: Theoretical approaches and the case of Greece. PhD thesis, Department of Economics, University of Crete, Rethymno.

Sotiropoulou I. (2012b). Economic activity without official currency in Greece: The * hypothesis. *International Journal of Community Currency Research*, 16, D70–9.

Sotiropoulou I. (2012c). Marketing a vintage carpet in a free bazaar and other stories on/off value. Third International Conference in Political Economy: 'Political Economy and the Outlook of Capitalism', Paris, France, 5–8 July. AHE, IIPPE & FAPE.

Sotiropoulou I. (2013). Terms of the Cretan dialect for non-monetary transactions. In Valeontis C. (ed.), *Hellenic Language and Terminology, conference proceedings*. ELETO, 281–93.

Sotiropoulou I. (2014a). Women in alternative economy, or what do women do without official currency? *Women's Studies International Forum*, 47, 339–48.

Sotiropoulou I. (2014b). Information and communication technologies in transactions: A question reversed. Online magazine *Απόψεις /Views/Apopseis* (special issue: Actions of social self organisation and internet), 41–6.

Sotiropoulou I. (2015a). Prices in parallel currency: The case of the exchange network of Chania, Crete. *International Journal of Community Currency Research*, 19 (special issue), D128–36.

Sotiropoulou I. (2015b). Everyday practices in Greece in the shadow of property: Urban domination subverted (?). In Allen A., Lampis A. & Swilling M. (eds), *Untamed urbanisms*. Taylor & Francis, 270–83.

Sotiropoulou I. (2016a). Solidarity, grassroots initiatives and power relations. *World Economic Review*, 6, 44–59.

Sotiropoulou I. (2016b). Collective viewings of value(s) and the struggle for what is valuable: The case of grassroots initiatives. *World Review of Political Economy*, 7(1), 56–84.

Sotiropoulou I. (2017). Absolute values, zero prices: An economic paradox as class war weapon, 10th International Critical Management Studies conference: 'Time for another revolution?', 35th Stream: Political economy, value & valuation: Advancing contemporary critiques of capitalism and exploring alternatives. Liverpool, 3–5 July.

Sotiropoulou I. (2019). Research and the elephant in the room: Encountering with violence in fieldwork concerning unpaid labour. In Wheatley D. (ed.), *Handbook of research methods on the quality of working lives*. Edward Elgar Publishing, 79–93.

Sotiropoulou I. (2020a). Quantity and social and solidarity economy: A quest for appropriate quantitative methods. *Review of Economics and Economic Methodology*, 4 (special issue: The methodology of economics: How mathematicians explain – or should they?), 131–56.

Sotiropoulou I. (2020b). Women in solidarity economy in Greece: Liberation practices or one more task undertaken by women?. In M. d. l. A. Di Capua M. d. l. A., Senent Vidal M. J. & Fajardo Garcia G. (eds), *Economia Solidaria y Social y Genero: Aportes Transdisciplinarios de Europa y America Latina (Social and solidarity economy and gender: Transdisciplinary contributions from Europe and Latin America)*. Tirant lo Blanch, 109–46.

Supiot A. (2017). *Governance by numbers: The making of a legal model of allegiance*. Trans. S. Brown. Hart Publishing.

The Sarai Programme (2003). Sarai Reader 03: Shaping technologies. The Sarai Programme CSDS, Delhi & The Waag Society/for Old and New Media Amsterdam, February.

Trejo Mendez P. (2020). Our bodies are not machines: From crisis to collective healing. *Convivial Thinking*, 14 June. Last accessed on 18 October 2022, https://convivialthinking.org/index.php/2020/06/14/bodies/

Trenkle N. (2014). Value and crisis: Basic questions. In Brown N., Larsen N., Nilgen M. & Robinson J. (eds), *Marxism and the critique of value*. M-C-M' Publishing, 1–16.

van den Berge J., Boelen R. & Vos, J. (2019). Citizen mobilization for water: The case of Thessaloniki, Greece. In Sultana F. & Loftus A. (eds), *Water politics: Governance, justice and the right to water*. Routledge, 161–74.

Velegrakis G., Andritsos T. & Poulios D. (2015). Uneven development: Lessons from the ongoing Greek tragedy. *Human Geography*, 8(3), 79–82.

Velupillai K. V. (2005). The unreasonable ineffectiveness of mathematics in economics. *Cambridge Journal of Economics*, 29(6), 849–72.

Von Werlhof C. (2007). No critique of capitalism without a critique of patriarchy! Why the left is no alternative. *Capitalism Nature Socialism*, 18(1), 13–27.

Waring M. (1999). *Counting for nothing: What men value and what women are worth*. Second edition. University of Toronto Press.

Weiner A. (1980). Reproduction: A replacement for reciprocity. *American Ethnologist*, 7(1), 71–85.

Weiner A. (1992). *Inalienable possessions*. University of California Press.

Wilmott P. & Orrell D. (2017). *The money formula: Dodgy finance, pseudo science, and how mathematicians took over the markets*. John Wiley & Sons.

Yeung K. (2018). Algorithmic regulation: A critical interrogation. *Regulation & Governance*, 12(4), 505–23.

Zelizer V. A. (1994). *Pricing the priceless child: The changing social value of children*. Princeton University Press.

Ziarek K. (1998). Powers to be: Art and technology in Heidegger and Foucault. *Research in Phenomenology*, 28(1), 162–94.

Zuboff S. (2019). *The age of surveillance capitalism: The fight for a human future at the new frontier of power*. Profile Books.

Index

164 *Index*

perception of value 20, 39, 60, 67,
71–2, 113–14, 133
physician 35, 50, 59, 65–9
platform 41, 48, 76, 79–83, 85, 90,
94, 118
police 29–30, 104, 107, 109–10
policing 29, 107
poor 5, 19, 23–4, 104, 128–9, 132
poverty 14, 34, 93, 98, 103–6, 112,
123, 130, 132, 134
precarious – precarity 101, 105–6,
132
precise – precision 34–5, 51–2, 53–4,
62, 69, 71, 82, 85, 90–1, 96, 98,
112, 117
prevailing economic system 14, 23,
25, 139
priceless 28, 71, 109
price 17, 28, 49–2, 61, 69–72, 92, 97,
108–9, 112–15, 122, 131–3
pricing 49–51, 86, 109, 113, 122
prioritization 8, 22, 28
priority 6, 17, 29, 51, 70, 82–3, 98,
113, 119, 129
privatization 104–5, 107–9, 122
privilege 53, 59, 66, 77, 121, 135
producer 14, 48, 50, 89, 91–2, 106,
128, 131, 133
production (process) 7, 14, 17,
19–24, 27–9, 31, 41, 57–64,
66–9, 72, 85–6, 89, 91–2, 94–7,
106, 113–15, 117, 119, 123,
125, 128–34, 136, 140, 142
productive 7, 18–19, 20, 73
profit 5–6, 8, 16–17, 18, 21, 28, 77,
92–3, 114, 118, 129, 135
property 15–7, 19–20, 63
public property 107–8
public expenditure cuts 104–5, 107
public service 105, 107–8
purpose 5, 20–2, 29, 40–1, 45, 48,
55, 80–1, 83, 86, 94, 97, 124,
128–30, 135, 139–41

quantification 3–4, 10–11, 13,
19–20, 27, 29–36, 42, 45,
49–51, 53, 72, 85, 93–4, 108,
110, 112, 116–17, 123, 136,
138–40
quantify 3, 21, 23, 28–9, 30–1, 34, 36,
45, 96, 115, 117
quantitative 10, 19, 21, 25, 28–9, 37,
40–3, 52, 54, 57, 121
quantity 1, 3–4, 8–11, 19, 25, 28,
30–2, 34–6, 41–2, 45, 49–52,
54, 57, 85–6, 91, 108, 112,
115–17, 121–2, 132, 135, 137,
140
reciprocity 54, 71, 90
redistribute – redistribution 60
refugee 8, 84–6
remuneration – remunerated 53, 59,
62–3, 69–70, 91, 98, 105, 112,
131–2
replication 16, 50, 131
reproduce – reproducing 18–19,
22–3, 25, 27–8, 36, 50,
68, 73, 96, 112, 116, 127,
135, 141
reproduction 11, 18, 20, 22–4, 27,
59, 106, 118–19, 125, 133–5,
140–1
reproduction crisis 23, 103,
social reproduction 22, 101, 103,
111, 122–4
research 3, 10, 13, 37–42, 47, 57, 71,
75, 77, 80–3, 116, 118–20,
141–2
research methods 37, 40
research participants 40–2, 50,
55, 58, 60–1, 72, 75, 86–7, 116,
119–20, 131, 136–7
researcher 10, 80–1, 118, 141
resistance 29–30, 32, 98, 104, 109–10,
133
rule(s) 7, 15, 53–5, 61, 70, 132

www.ingramcontent.com/pod-product-compliance
Lightning Source LLC
Chambersburg PA
CBHW061740270326
41928CB00011B/2321